1966

THE YEAR OF

THE HORSE

Robert K. Powers

First published by Dog Ear Publishing
4010 W. 86th Street, Ste H
Indianapolis, IN 46268
www.dogearpublishing.net

ISBN: 978-160844-202-7
Library of Congress Control Number: 2009942051

This book is printed on acid-free paper.

Printed in the United States of America

Index

About the Author

Bob Powers is a native Chicagoan and was raised on the south side of Chicago in the Brainerd neighborhood. He is a journeyman electrician and a longtime member of I.B.E.W. Local 134. In January 1966, the Chinese Year of the Horse, he was drafted into the Army. He had infantry training at Tigerland, Ft. Polk, Louisiana and was assigned to the 7th Cavalry, 1st Air Cavalry Division in Vietnam.

The following nine months were spent in combat. On May 18, 1967, he was severely wounded in Quang Ngai province near Duc Pho. The next several months, he was in a series of Army hospitals with surgeries and orthopedic rehabilitation. Discharged in 1968, he returned to his trade. He is married and has four grown children and resides in Mokena, Illinois.

Dedication

I would like to dedicate this writing to all the men that I served with and in particular to those who made the supreme sacrifice, and to family members SP4 Thomas P. O'Dea and SSgt. Lawrence C. Rose who made that sacrifice.

To my mother, Frances Rita, who was my strength, and through her faith and prayers, I made it home. She was the real soldier.

Acknowledgements

I would like to thank the members of the Mokena Library Writers Group for their support and a very special thanks to Phyllis Jacobek, Library Director, and Shirley Guendling, Writers Group Moderator.

Preface

It took me many years to sit down and write my story. It was a long time before I even felt comfortable talking about my experiences let alone writing about them.

When I was discharged in March of 1968, it was a very chaotic time. Soon afterward, the Kennedy-King assassinations, the rioting at the Democratic National Convention in Chicago and the Kent State University incident made things even worse. All the anti-war demonstrations and dissention about the Vietnam War, stirred even more emotion. People were spitting on the returning troops at Oakland and calling them "baby killers." After they had sacrificed so much, they expected to be treated with the respect and dignity of previous returning veterans. What a shock then to be greeted by this. Some people had forgotten that these men were their soldiers doing what their country asked them to do as so many had done in the past wars and service.

Many of the young men of that time were very concerned with how to avoid Vietnam. Draft eligible men were getting married in order to change their draft status. Later on, it became necessary to be married with children to meet the criteria. I have often wondered how many of these marriages failed. Two of my friends did exactly that with their parents' encouragement and both of their marriages failed. If all else failed, there was always Canada or draft lawyers.

In September of 1968, a family member was killed in action at Darlac, Vietnam while serving with the 4th Inf. Division. He was buried with full military honors. I attended his wake and funeral and saw first hand what the war could do to a family. Then in May of 1969, another family member was killed in action at Quang Ngai, Vietnam while serving with the 11th Light Inf. Brigade. Ironically Quang Ngai was the very same place where I had almost lost my own life two years to the month and week earlier.

I remember how I felt at that time, wondering why I had survived and Larry and Tommy had not. I can still see my mother's face when she received those phone calls and staring at me with a mother's gratitude for her answered prayers and her extreme sorrow for those who had lost so much. Through the years that have past, I have come to the realization that there is only one explanation for who lived and who died; it just wasn't your time.

After all these events, and observing and listening to the opinions of the war all around me, I determined that my best course of action was to do my best to put the whole thing behind me and immerse myself into my work, family, and friends, and get on with my life. In retrospect, I think I made the right decision.

It was not until the Vietnam Veterans Parade in Chicago in 1986, that things began to change for the Vietnam Vets. The country began to realize the wrong that had been done to its soldiers who had served with honor. I am proud to say that I marched in that parade and it helped begin the healing process for many of us.

Recently, I have been encouraged by my family and friends to write this story. My story is very much the same as thousands of infantry soldiers who fought in Vietnam. I think what makes it a little unique is the people that I served with and telling the story through the eyes of a private.

CHAPTER 1

Late 1965

September of 1965 rolled into my life as a very happy time. I had just completed my apprenticeship in Local 134 of the I.B.E.W., and I was now a journeyman electrician. I can't begin to describe how much this meant to me. My grandfather and father were electricians, and from the time I was a little boy, this is what I wanted to be. I always loved tools and working with my hands. To build something and see it completed was my passion.

I had a new 421 Pontiac Bonneville coupe and a Corvette powered cherry '56 Chevy. I loved muscle cars and drag racing. My love life was great and my future was looking good.

There was only one thing that was ahead of me and that was my military obligation. Being an electrical apprentice, I had a class 1Y student deferment. Upon the completion of my apprenticeship training, my classification reverted back to 1A and draft eligible status.

The Vietnam War was heating up and so were the draft numbers. It was time for me to make a decision as to what my course was to be.

At this time, my older brother was in the Army Reserves in a counter intelligence unit. He suggested that I join the reserves and avoid the two year hitch. I agreed that this was probably my best choice. He said that he would see if he could get me into his reserve unit. He went to his battalion commander, Col. Tom Blanchard, and convinced him that with my electrical and electronic schooling, I would be an asset to an intelligence unit. The Colonel agreed to accept me as a candidate to the unit and he would schedule an interview with me.

One week later, I found myself driving down Garfield Boulevard heading to the 5th U.S. Army Headquarters in Hyde Park. When I arrived at the headquarters, I pulled into the parking area and found myself a good spot where no one would be bouncing doors off my car. This was my first new car and I was very particular about where it was parked.

The headquarters was housed in a beautiful old mansion surrounded by shady old trees and it had a superb view of Lake Michigan. The weather was just beautiful for this time of the year and the smell of the lake just did something to make you feel alive and well.

I walked up the steps to the veranda and into the foyer. There was a small information desk with a very neat looking soldier in attendance. I told him that I had an appointment with Col. Blanchard and he asked me to take a seat. I sat down on a large red leather couch and picked up a copy of the Chicago Sun Times and began to read. Vietnam was the front page news and the deployment of several Army divisions. General William Westmoreland was quoted as saying there would be a substantial manpower buildup. There was also a story about the success of the 1st Air Cavalry and the role that it was playing as the new Army concept strike force using helicopters.

I was still reading when I heard my name called. I looked up and Col. Blanchard was standing in front of me with his hand extended for a handshake.

He said, "Hi Robert, I'm Col. Blanchard. Jack has told me a lot about you."

I stood up and shook his hand and he directed me toward a long corridor which led to his office. I followed him into his office, and he pulled a chair up in front of his desk.

He said, "Please have a seat. Give me a moment and we'll get started." While he was gathering his paperwork, the phone rang and he answered with a brisk, "Col. Blanchard CIC." He motioned to me that he would only be a minute.

I looked around his office and saw framed citations, encased medals, and all kinds of personal memorabilia. It was obvious to me that the Colonel had been around in his Army career.

He completed his phone call and hung the phone up and looked over at me and shook his head.

"You'll have to excuse me, this place is a nuthouse of activity today. Our unit just completed summer camp at Camp McCoy, and I'm working on our new schedule for the fall meetings. Your brother tells me that you just completed an electrical apprenticeship which included one year of electronic schooling. Tell me a little about yourself, your training, and current employment?"

I proceeded to give him a brief rundown of my education, technical training, and employment. The whole while, the Colonel listened and occasionally interjected a question.

When I was done, he looked at me and said, "I believe we can use a young man with your background in our battalion. In counter intelligence, there is need for electronic surveillance and the like and that area is growing by leaps and bounds. I'll set up a physical exam at the induction center and let you know when it is. You don't look like you'll have any problem with the physical. I look forward to talking to you afterward and we'll work up a schedule for your basic training."

He stood and extended his hand and said, "Nice meeting you, Robert. I'll be in touch."

I left feeling that I had made a good impression. I was almost enthusiastic about my upcoming service.

One week to the day later, I got a phone call from Col. Blanchard.

"Robert, I've got your physical all set for Monday, the 27th of September at the Armed Forces Induction Center at 615 W. Van Buren at 6am. sharp. Did you get all that?"

"Yes sir," I responded, "I'll be there."

He acknowledged and said, "Good luck and I'll be in touch."

The 27th of September came around very quickly. I had to get up at 4:30 in order to make the 6:00 physical downtown. I caught the 5:12 Rock Island train bound for LaSalle Street Station. It was barely light outside and it was raining a little. I got off the train and started to walk west on Van Buren Street. It was only a few city blocks to the induction center. It was raining very hard when I arrived at the center, and I was soaked to the skin.

There were lots of young guys heading through the door. Inside it was a typical government building, very plain and devoid of color and windows. A burly looking soldier was standing near the door shouting orders at everyone coming in. I knew this was not going to be a fun day. He had us all line up against the wall and told us to look down at the floor and observe the 4 inch yellow line on the floor. He instructed the lead person to follow the yellow line to the next station with the rest of us in tow.

At the next station, everyone was seated in chair desks where we filled out our preliminary paperwork. Then, we were back on the yellow line and on to the next station where the physical began in earnest. A basket was provided for our clothing and we were told to strip naked and place our clothing in the basket and move on to the next station. Now, here we all are buck naked, following the yellow line through the next several stations. I found this to be the most embarrassing and degrading situation that I'd ever been in but I suppose it had to be that way in order to process so many people every day.

We were checked for everything imaginable and then allowed to get dressed and turn in our baskets. This day was my first experience with military lines and the old Army cliché: "hurry up and wait." There would be many more lines in my future.

After a horrible free lunch that was barely edible, we were back on the yellow line and into the chair desks for a battery of tests which took a couple hours. At the end of the testing, we were separated into groups and told to wait for our names to be called.

After an hour or so, my name was called and I was led to the desk of Capt. William Hart. He had my papers in front of him and he was in the process of signing them.

He looked up at me and said, "You are rejected and all the reasons are in this paperwork. You are released and you may go."

I went out the door in a state of shock. As I walked down the street, I thought to myself, who cares? I didn't really want to go into the Army anyway. I caught the 3:10 train back to Brainerd Station.

Riding along on the train, I looked at my paperwork to see why I was rejected. The first reason was unstable collateral ligaments of the right knee. The second reason was an abnormality of the lower spine and the final reason was flat feet. I had injured my right knee about nine years previously but I thought it was fine. With all these things wrong with me, that's the end of my military obligation.

That evening at the dinner table, I told my brother what had happened at the physical.

He said, "Well that takes care of that. I'll let Col. Blanchard know what happened."

It sure felt good to have the burden of my military obligation out of the way. Now I could get on with my life. This was cause for a celebration so I hopped in my car and went off to my local hangout on Ashland Avenue, Johnny O's Cocktail Lounge.

Johnny O's was a nice quiet comfortable place with soft indirect lighting on a real neat blue cove ceiling. There were comfortable red leather booths and no loud pinball games that could attract the wrong type of customers. It was the kind of place that you could bring a date and there wouldn't be any problems.

John was a good guy and could always provide some lively conversation. He was a WWII Navy veteran and he had been around the block a few times so he always had some good advice for me. John and I spent many an evening discussing all manner of topics. He had an uncanny ability to show me another point of view.

All my friends liked Johnny O's as well, so I was always in good company. If you happened to be hungry, there was an open gas grill behind the bar and John offered a large burger with all the trimmings that was cooked to your specification and never a disappointment.

As I walked into the lounge, John gave me his usual greeting while he reached for a bottle Old Style.

"How did you make out with your physical? Are you packing yet? My business is going to take a big hit," he said laughingly.

I told him what had happened.

"What a relief, I was going to start doing this place in purple and black bunting."

A couple of friends of mine came in and before long we were into our normal talk of jobs, cars, and girls. That was the great thing about Johnny O's, everyone knew everyone and we all got along great. Several of us had gone to grammar school together and we were all still in our beloved neighborhood. Little did any of us realize, but things were about to change in a big way for all of us.

The next two months were uneventful but good. Work was plentiful and everyone seemed to be doing pretty well. As December and the Christmas holidays came closer, the headlines of the newspapers were Vietnam and more Vietnam. The casualties were on the rise and more troops were being brought in. The Army had five combat divisions there and they were looking for more. The Marine numbers were also on the rise. South Korea sent two combat divisions as well, the Tiger and White Horse Divisions. The U.S. was bombing North Vietnam with the hope of slowing down enemy supplies to the south.

All my friends were at that twenty-two year old mark so the draft was a major topic. Everyone was trying to figure out what was going to happen and what move to make. I, on the other hand, was out of that picture, or so I thought, so I was offering my advice to them. Ironically, I was the only one in our group that would ever see Vietnam.

CHAPTER 2

January 1966

J anuary 1966, the Chinese year of the horse, I didn't know it at the time but this was to have great meaning for me and was also the beginning of strange numerical coincidences and premonitions that would follow me for the next two years. Over the years, I have become convinced that these things do have some kind of meaning but I don't know what.

On January 10, my deceased father's birthday, I received a notice for a physical for the draft. I found that to be a bit strange seeing how I was rejected in September. Maybe it was standard procedure. I would make certain that I brought my rejection papers with me and maybe I'd only be there a short time and not to have to go through the whole routine again. I had to report to the induction center on the 24th of January at 6:00am. I wasn't real concerned for the next two weeks, especially when I thought about the fact that I was rejected for three different reasons.

The 24th arrived and I was back on the 5:12 Rock Island train bound for LaSalle Street Station and the induction center.

I arrived at the center right on time and found it to be much more crowded than it was the time before. I got to the preliminary paperwork station and went to the person in charge and submitted my rejection papers. He informed me that previous testing for other branches of service had nothing to do with the draft physical and testing, so I would have to do it all over again. That sure didn't make my day but there was nothing I could do about it.

I went through the whole routine again. At the last station, I was told that I was accepted. I was in shock but I was glad that I had brought my papers with me. I asked to see the person in charge and I was happy to see that it was Capt. William Hart, the same officer who had signed my rejection papers. I handed him the rejection paper expecting that he would void this test.

He looked them over and said to me, "You have been accepted and you will be drafted." I asked how that could be after I had been rejected just four months prior.

He sarcastically replied, "Everyone makes mistakes," as he handed my papers back to me. This was bad news but there was still more to come.

I finished the day out at the center and left for home. My mind was racing with the confusion of how I could fail a physical for three different reasons and all of a sudden I'm just fine and about to be drafted. The best thing that I could do was to contact Col. Blanchard and let him know that I'm now acceptable for service.

The next day I called the colonel and explained the whole situation to him. He told me that once you are accepted on a draft physical that you are scheduled for induction and cannot enlist in any other branch of the Armed Forces. The only other option would be to try and fight the physical legally or to just let the draft take its course and see if I could luck out.

I thought the whole situation over and decided that I really didn't like the idea of meetings and summer camp for the whole six year obligation so I elected to let the draft go through and get it out of the way. I was convinced that with the schooling that I had in the electrical field that I would be useful to the Army in some way other than "romp and stomp." I also was aware of the fact that it takes six support soldiers for every combat soldier. The Army had many other jobs and duty stations beside Vietnam. I felt that the three problems that were discovered on my first physical were true and that would greatly reduce my chances of being a foot soldier. I was beginning to like the odds. I even started to like the idea of the two year hitch and no summer camp and meetings.

I had a few friends that had pushed up their draft or enlisted in the service after high school and were now discharged. I sought out their advice and they all agreed that there was a real good chance that I would probably get some type of MOS or job that would be okay and complete the two year hitch with no problem. They had all done okay and were none the worse for wear.

That being settled, I needed to put my affairs in order. First, there were my two cars. I would have to sell my Bonneville to get rid of the car payment and I also would have to sell my Chevy because I had no place to store it while I was away. I worked out a deal with my brother where I took his '61 Pontiac convertible and cash for the Bonneville. Then I sold my Chevy to Bert Weber, a neighborhood acquaintance, for $700.00. I almost cried when I sold the car as I had built it from a plain six cylinder stick shift to a 375 horsepower, fuel injected 327, floor shifting machine. The car only had 20K miles on it and I had it custom painted and put a new interior in it. I was so proud of that car and the work that I had done on it. The car was better than new. When I would go out, it was a fun decision as to which car I was going to drive; one was as sharp as the other and that was a time when cars were a big deal.

The night that Bert came to pick the Chevy up, I had the car parked out in front of the house and it was sparkling clean. He paid me and I handed him the title, bill of sale, and the keys. He wished me good luck in the service.

We shook hands and he said, "Don't worry, Bob, I'll take good care of it."

He went out the door and down the front steps and hopped in his new car. I heard the deep rumble of the tuned exhaust as it started up and I watched it pull away into the night. I never saw the car again.

The next thing that I had to do was inform my contractor that I would be leaving their employ in the near future. At the time, I was working for Westinghouse Electric. I had served my apprenticeship with them. I was working at the Daley Center in downtown Chicago and had worked on the building all through its construction. The superintendent was a man by the name of Dave Connors.

Dave was one of the finest men that I've ever known in the electrical industry. He had been my first foreman and had taught me a lot of the things that would carry me through forty-seven active years in the trade. I told Dave of my plight and he told me to do what I had to do and my job would be waiting for me when I returned. He told me that he would miss me and that he had big plans for me but he was sure that there would be other plans in two years.

My draft notice arrived at the very end of February and my induction date was the 30th of March 1966. They sure didn't waste any time. The next month flew by and the end of March was approaching. It was time to start saying goodbye to all my friends and relatives. There were a couple of going-away parties for me and all of a sudden it was the 29th of March and time for me to pack my bag. I didn't have to pack much. All I needed was the basic toiletries and the clothes on my back and the Army would take it from there.

Once again I found myself on the 5:12am train heading toward downtown Chicago and the induction center. I'll always remember that walk down Van Buren to the induction center. It was dark and misting and I remember hoping this was not a bad omen. Oh how I hated this place. The good news was that I'd never see it again.

When I arrived there, I was placed into a group of about fifty young men.

I was standing amongst the group when I heard someone say, "Hey Bob, they got you too!"

I turned around and I saw a tall curly haired guy walking toward me. It was Bob Olejniczak. I knew Bob from grammar school at St. Kilian. We shook hands and I instantly felt better knowing that now I wasn't alone in this.

He said to me, "This really sucks. I suppose we're on the express train to Vietnam."

I replied, "I sure hope not. I was kind of hoping for some nice cushy job in Europe or Stateside."

I hadn't seen Bob since 1957 so we had a lot of ground to cover in between the processing stations and testing. The day actually went by pretty quickly.

The next process was taking the oath. We were herded into a large room where an Army officer administered the oath of allegiance. We were now officially and legally members of the U.S. Armed Forces and subject to both civil and military law.

There was a Marine sergeant standing to our front and he ordered us to line up around the room against the wall. A husky little guy pushed his way in between me and the guy to my left.

He looked at me apologetically and said, "Sorry buddy, I just want to stick with my friend here. We're doing the buddy system."

I nodded.

The Marine sergeant bellowed out, "Eighteen of you sorry assed f....rs are going into the Marine Corps. Don't bother moving away or changing places because every day I change my selection method. Today it's every other man!"

With that, he quickly pulled every other man forward to include the guy on my left and my right. The guy that squeezed his way in was now a Marine. He immediately started to squeal and explain to the Marine sergeant that he had traded places with me and that he wanted to be with his friend on the buddy system.

The sergeant roared back at him, "Shut up you little weasel and get over there with those other losers. From now on the Marine Corps will be the only buddy that you'll be needing!"

He herded the eighteen prospective marines out the door and there were tears streaming down the little guys face. I could imagine how he felt being separated from his friend. After that, we all stood around talking and saying that we were lucky not to be part of that group.

About ten minutes passed and the door burst open and here comes the Marine sergeant again and screaming, "Guess what? I need one more warm body!"

Everyone started to head toward the other side of the room trying to put as much distance between the sergeant and themselves as possible. By now the sergeant was really enjoying himself. He walked right directly up to me and for a second we were eye to eye.

Suddenly he barked, "You back in the corner; that's right you; get up here. You're in the Corps. Follow me." He led the young man away.

We received our service numbers and were told that we would be doing our basic training at Ft. Polk, Louisiana. Transportation for our departure would be arranged later that same day.

A short time later, we were loaded on two buses and transported to O'Hare International Airport for a flight to Alexandria, Louisiana. Our flight was on a Flying Tiger Airline DC3. The plane was old and rickety.

I looked over at Bob and said, "Do you think this old tub will make it to Louisiana?" Just at that moment, the engines fired up and we could see blue smoke belching out of the exhaust ports.

Bob said to me, "This is scary. I don't like flying, especially on an old piece of shit like this."

It was a four hour flight on the bucket of bolts but we made it okay. When we got to Alexandria, there was another bus ride to Ft. Polk. Everyone was pretty tired when we arrived. It took awhile before we were able to settle in get some sleep at the replacement depot.

North Ft. Polk had just reopened for the Vietnam surge and special training. North Ft. Polk came into existence when the Army was segregated and was originally built for black soldiers. The North Fort had not been used since the Korean Conflict and was in sad shape. After a few days of processing, clothing, immunizing, and the like, we began what the Army calls zero week.

Due to the condition of the company area and billeting, we spent the next two weeks cleaning all the buildings, painting, building sidewalks, and almost anything else imaginable to make this place livable for basic training. We worked ten hours a day. The heat during the day was intense. The tops of both of my ears blistered from the heat. This was the only time and place that this ever happened to me. It was not a very pleasant experience to say the least.

When the work was completed, the area became E Company, 3rd Battalion, 5th Training Brigade and I was now Pvt. E1 Robert Powers US55887711. My service number was all pairs and each of the four numbers would become part of the numerical coincidences that would follow me over the next two years.

Basic training began in earnest. Everything was what I expected it to be except for the Louisiana weather. It would get very cold and damp at night and Army regulations require that all windows in the barracks be kept open six inches during the night. There was lots of shivering at night even with two wool blankets. The humidity made the sheets and blankets feel wet and then with the temperature drop at night it was cold. The mornings were cold and by noon the heat was so intense and you couldn't wait until lunch time so that you could shed the field jacket. The weather in Louisiana was very similar to Vietnam. Both were just plain miserable.

There was a spinal meningitis scare at Ft. Polk so there were no passes issued during basic training and that didn't go over too well. It would be twelve weeks before we would see any leave time.

Beside Bob Olejniczak, there were about half dozen or so guys from Chicago and we all hung out together because we had a lot in common. Bob Olejniczak was a character. He had a very sarcastic funny wit about him and he kept me laughing all the time. Some of his expressions and reactions were hysterical. He absolutely hated the Army and he was always searching for the easy way out and, of course, there was none.

Every chance we got, he and I would be sprawled out in the shade smoking cigarettes. In the Army, you quickly learn that when they call "take five," you light up whether you smoked or not or you might be grabbed for some other detail. We were on to that real fast.

We knew a lot of the same guys and girls from the Brainerd and Gresham neighborhoods in Chicago so we were always swapping tales and teasing each other.

We went through all the normal training of physical therapy, rifle range, bayonet training, close combat, live fire range, bivouac and all that good stuff.

Drill instructors were screaming at us all day and telling us: "You better give your soul to God 'cuz your ass belongs to me."

They would tell us that they would rather have a daughter a whore than a son at Ft. Polk or if you were going to give the United States an enema you would be sticking the tube in it at Ft. Polk. Another of my all time favorites was when we were in the mess hall and trying to eat.

They would be yelling, "Eat fast and haul ass" or "Shut up, eat, and get out." "You're not home with your mama now and Jody is doin' your girl friend while you're gone."

I have to admit that the time flew by. We were now about two weeks away from completing basic and the rumors were flying about what was going to take place when our orders for advanced training came down. I still felt that I was going to get lucky and draw something decent.

One night in the barracks this little guy, Petrocelli, was voicing his opinion of what was going to happen.

He said, "We're all going for infantry training and we're all going to Nam."

I was getting tired of listening to him orate about this so I said to him, "That's a bunch of bull shit. There is going to be lots of different jobs and people going every which way. It takes six troops to support one combat soldier."

By now we were in a heated argument and he was getting madder by the minute. Guys were taking my side because they were sick of listening to his shit too.

I said, "You say we are all going infantry. There are forty guys in our platoon and I got twenty bucks that says no more than twenty will be infantry."

"You're on. That's the easiest twenty I'll ever make," he snapped.

Twenty bucks was a weeks pay for us so I hoped that I was right because I really didn't need to lose a double sawbuck right before leave.

The day of the order posting arrived and we all crowded around the outside bulletin board to see what assignments we had. As I neared the board, Bob Olejniczak was moving away.

He looked at me and said, "You don't wanna know." He looked really disgusted.

"This time we really got screwed. Take a look!"

I scanned the alphabetical list until I came to his name. It said 11B – light weapons infantry – Ft. Polk, Louisiana. I jumped down to my name and it read 11C – indirect fire crewman – Ft. Polk, Louisiana. This was terrible news. It meant we were both in the infantry and what was worse we would receive our training at Tigerland, Ft. Polk.

Everybody who trained at Tigerland was headed for Vietnam as soon as they could get you there. There was more bad news. Since we were reassigned to Ft. Polk, we wouldn't receive any travel pay so our round trip to Chicago for leave would be out of our pockets. The only good news that day was that I won the twenty dollar bet with Petrocelli and that little shit was selected to be a clerk typist and to take his training on the west coast so who really won?

We started making our plans to go home for our two week leave and decided the fastest way home would be for a bunch of us Chicago boys to pool together and take a cab to New Orleans and then go standby to Chicago. Bob Olejniczak, John Wnek, Tony Turano, Ed Metz, and I made arrangements with a cab driver for the big escape. We couldn't wait to get out of Polk and Louisiana. We were all sick of the weather and being away from home. We really never got to see anything except the post as seen from the back of a deuce and half truck. Out of our little group, everyone except Tony would be coming back to Polk for infantry training.

Everything went great with our cab ride to New Orleans. The scenery along the highway was beautiful although no one would admit it. All we ever said about Louisiana is that we didn't ever want to come back although we'd be back alright. The cabbie was quite a character. He gave us the whole history of the area from Lake Charles to New Orleans. Story after story, he kept us laughing and we sure needed that after the past twelve weeks of misery.

As we passed through a little town called Ville Platte, he pointed out some little white frame cottages and a bar nestled in among moss covered cypress trees. It looked like your typical red neck bar; the kind that you backed into so they thought you were leaving.

He said, "You boys lookin' ta have a lil' fun 'fore we get to N'Orleans? That there's the finest lil' cat house in this part of Louisiana. They got high yellas, creoles, brown sugar, and white bitches too! All of 'em real lookers. All the regulars from Polk come down here 'specially after pay day. You boys look like you could do with some ass! How long since you took a roll in the hay?"

It got real quiet in the cab as everyone started thinking and counting. One thing was for sure, none of us wanted to stop and mess around. All we wanted was to get to the New Orleans Airport, get on standby, and catch the earliest flight to Chicago that we possibly could. We thanked him none the less and told him maybe some other time. He probably was on their payroll for finder fees.

The cabbie got us to the airport safe and quicker than we expected so we all threw in a couple extra bucks and thanked him again. We all got lucky and made the first flight out and to make it even better we were in 1st class. A pretty little stewardess seated us and of course Bob O. had plenty of one liners and had her laughing. I think she liked him because she took extra good care of us. What a thrill to have someone cater to your needs after what we had just been through and especially someone as pretty as her.

Bob ordered a beer and I got myself a VO and water. These were the first real drinks that we had since leaving Chicago. All they had on post was 3% beer which was one notch better than nothing. Bob called it moose piss.

I said to Bob, "What are you going to do on leave?"

He laughed and said, "I'm going to sleep late everyday and drink as much cold beer as I can. I'm going to spend as much time as I can with my girlfriend and have sex three times a day. How about you?"

I replied, "Probably the same as you. I don't have a girl right now so I'll probably just be doing a lot of partying. Two weeks isn't much time to get something going and what girl wants a guy in the Army?"

My brother picked Bob and I up at O'Hare and we headed south down the Kennedy expressway.

I said to Bob, "I used to own this car, believe it or not."

He said, "You know, I saw this car before. I remember it because of the twin spotlights but I never knew it was yours. This is one sharp car. I love Bonnevilles. Have you got any wheels now?"

I said, "Yeah, I've got a '61 Pontiac Catalina convertible. My brother and I did a little trading and worked it out. My neighbor is going to let me store the car in his garage while I'm away."

He said, "I had a nice Chevelle but I had no where to go with it so I had to sell it. The damn thing was almost paid for too! I would have left it with my girlfriend but it was a four speed and she didn't know how to drive anyway."

We dropped Bob off at his parents' house in Gresham and I told him to call me the last weekend of leave and we'd hook up for our return trip to Ft. Polk.

I said, "See you in two weeks. Have fun!"

As we rolled up in front of the house, I saw my mom and my aunt Helen sitting outside with our next door neighbors, Bill and Sue Kerwin. Sitting outside and talking to the neighbors was a great Chicago summer ritual. Neighbors were close almost like extended family. I always made time for the neighbors and we all watched out for each other. Most Chicago neighborhoods were like that.

Everyone had hugs and greetings for me. It was great to be home and yet in a way it felt strange because I knew in two weeks that I'd have to leave again. I ran through a brief summary of the food and training. I left out the part about Tigerland being the next stop before Vietnam. Maybe the conflict would be settled by the time I got there or maybe with a little luck or a whole lot of luck, I'd be assigned elsewhere. That was to be very wishful thinking.

It was June and the weather was great. I had so many people to see and had more plans than I could ever squeeze into two weeks. The time went by so fast I couldn't believe it. When I was down at Polk in training, the days seemed so much longer especially when you were doing something that you didn't like which was most of the time.

I did manage to have a lot of fun and I met a nice girl in the process which was a plus. Her name was Kathleen. She had long dark hair and a devilish bright smile. She was petite and had a cute shape. She knew how to flirt and be funny. It had been quite a while since I had any kind of relationship and she most definitely had a great personality and was largely responsible for the fun that I had on leave. She was four years younger than me and I think that fascinated her a little and the fact that I knew and hung out with her older brother contributed a little. Kathleen knew how to make me feel good and if ever there was a time for it, this was it.

Throughout my entire life, I never had any age barriers. If I liked someone, age had nothing to do with it. I always related to older people and their wisdom and with younger people I always tried to steer them in the right direction.

My last Saturday at home arrived and most of it was spent saying goodbye to everyone. The good news was that I'd be back in two months for another visit.

Bob Olejniczak called me and said, "You ready to go back to Ft. Puke?"

"Hell no, I'm just starting to have some real fun. How about you?" I responded.

"Going back to that hellhole, is enough to depress anyone. Shoulda went to Canada."

He gave me a rundown of what he did with his leave time and it sounded like he had a good time too. I told him that I had transportation arranged for our trip to O'Hare the next day. My brother was going to drive us and the rest of the return trip was already pre-arranged.

Bob said, "Can you imagine how miserable Fort Polk will be in July and August. If the damn heat and training don't get us then the bugs and snakes will!"

I replied, "I guess we'll have to just grin and bear it. We sure don't have any choice in the matter but maybe lady luck will come our way. Anyway we'll pick you up at your house at 2:00 tomorrow. See you then."

CHAPTER 3

Tigerland

My brother and I picked Bob up as scheduled on Sunday afternoon and we began our ride to O'Hare Airport to catch a standby flight in the direction of Ft. Polk. We said thanks and goodbye to my brother and he wished us good luck.

We went into the main lobby and over to the information center. There was a little red-haired cutie sitting at the desk and we explained that we were looking for a standby flight to New Orleans.

Seeing us in uniforms, she said, "Heading for Ft. Polk, guys?"

We responded affirmatively and she had a great suggestion. She recommended that we try for a Braniff Airline 4:37 flight to Shreveport and that there was a bus line that would take us right to Ft. Polk. This was fantastic because it cut our travel expenses by more than half of what we had anticipated. We made all our arrangements with Braniff including the bus ride.

It was only 3:20 so we had a little time to kill so we headed into a nice little bar right off the main terminal which was real close to the Braniff gates. We each ordered an Old Style and we started talking about our training and what our futures might hold. We both knew that things didn't look too good but we had to hope something good would happen. We had time for a second round and then we headed over to gate D16 and checked in with the attendant and she told us that there would be no problem making the flight on standby so we grabbed a seat in the waiting area until we were called.

It was a short uneventful flight to Shreveport and we made our bus connection at the airport with no problem. The bus trip was longer than our flight but we were in no hurry to get back to Ft. Polk. We were both tired from the day so we kicked back and caught a little sleep.

The bus rolled into north fort at 10:45 and we made our way to F Company, 1st Battalion, 3rd Training Brigade and the CQ building. We dropped our duffel bags outside the door and went in. A corporal was seated at one of the desks with a goose necked light focused on the latest copy of Playboy magazine.

He looked up at us as if we were an annoyance and said, "Suppose you two slick sleeves are looking for your barracks. What's yer names?"

We told him and he flipped through the company roster and looked up at us.

"You're both in fourth platoon. It's the last barracks down the road. Grab any bunk you want. Your platoon sergeant will reorganize you tomorrow."

We grabbed our bags and hoisted them up on our shoulders and walked down the road to 4th platoon barracks. It was a typical WWII wooden two story frame building. The platoon was housed on the 1st floor and NCO's on the 2nd floor. There was a big latrine on the left as you went in the door. There were six shower heads in one big stall, six sinks lined up next to each other, six thunder mugs with no partitions, and one urinal trough. The bunks were out in the bay area and they were doubles with ten on each side to house the forty man platoon. There were two rooms on the very end of the bay for the drill sergeant and his assistant.

We grabbed the first empty double bunk we came across. I took the top and Bob took the bottom. There were about thirty guys already settled in. We introduced ourselves to the guys around us and started to put our clothes into the foot and wall lockers.

Our two friends from Chicago hadn't arrived yet but they probably came via New Orleans and that would take longer. It was well after midnight when we finally stretched out on the bare mattresses and closed our eyes and fell asleep. I didn't get a lot of sleep as people were coming in throughout the night and talking. The lights were constantly going on and off. Finally about 3am, it quieted down and I drifted into a deep sleep.

At 5:30, I was awakened with a shock. This goofy sergeant flips the lights on and he's running up and down the bay clanging two garbage can lids on each other and hitting the bunk rails with them.

He's screaming, "Off your ass and on your feet! Outside in formation in twenty minutes or your sorry ass belongs to me!"

There was total chaos as forty guys hit the latrine and tried to get dressed and outside in formation. There was a lot of cussing and mumbling as we went through our moves. Bob and I managed to get outside but there were quite a few stragglers after the mark. I could see the smirk on the drill sergeant's face. He was a short muscular black man. He had a 173rd Airborne Division combat patch on his right arm and a CIB and Jump Wings above his shirt pocket. He had the drill instructor hat on and tipped up in the back. One look at this guy and you could tell he was in love with himself and was a real bad ass. He and his assistants lined us all up into formation and had us drop and give him fifty push-ups for being so slow.

He said, "My name's Sgt. Thomas. I'm your senior drill instructor. I'm the law here. It's my job to get you sorry-assed slugs ready for 'Nam in eight weeks. You got no idea what you're walkin' into over there but that's what this place is all about. I'm gonna be watchin' every move you make and you better f....n' well do it right. There are two rules at the top of the list; No. 1: you will have your steel pot on your head every waking minute of the f....n' day, No. 2: you will run everywhere you go. You will not get caught walkin' or you're in deep shit. Is that understood?"

The instructors ran us through a PT drill and a one mile run. That would be our normal starting routine and after a while the run distance would be extended. After the PT, we broke from formation and lined up by the mess hall and awaited some hot chow. One thing to be said about this type of a morning start is that you would be so hungry that you'd eat anything.

For the next order of business, the entire battalion of eight hundred troops was marched into a theater and seated. We figured it was probably for a training film or some other army propaganda. A Sergeant-Major walked out onto the stage and called us to attention and said to remain seated. A full bird Colonel followed and stepped up to the microphone.

"My name is Col. Jacobs. I am your brigade commander. I would like to welcome you all to Tigerland and to wish you all good luck with your training. I want you to know that every single man in front of me is going to Vietnam! Is there anyone in front of me who doubts this? Half of you are going to the 25th Infantry Division and the other half is going to the 1st Air Cavalry Division so it would behoove you to take this training very seriously. It could just make a difference in whether you live or die."

At that moment you could hear a pin drop in that theater. Everyone knew that this was no joke and that we had better take all the training seriously. I know for myself, this was a turning point.

There wasn't going to be any lucking out or any assignment in Europe, Korea, or anywhere! It was Vietnam like it or not. The Colonel spoke for another twenty minutes about Tigerland and how it was the best place and training to prepare for combat in Vietnam.

The balance of our first day was spent receiving our bedding and equipment. In other words, from one line and place to another.

Bob looked at me and said, "This really sucks! I guess we're in for it!"

I just nodded. It sure wasn't my happiest day and it seemed like everything was getting worse. I had a very real premonition that I was going to wind up in the 1st Cavalry.

We found out that our two Chicago buddies, Ed and John, were in the second platoon so we wouldn't be seeing as much of them .They were in a different barracks but they were at the same training sessions so we would see them there and after training hours.

We all fell into the daily routine of physical training, running a mile every morning and then the morning and afternoon training sessions. All of these sessions were Vietnam oriented even down to appearance. There were villages, booby traps, and cadre dressed in black pajamas, conical hats, and carrying AK47s. Most of our instructors had been through a tour in Vietnam or were experts in whatever field that we were training in. A lot of time was devoted to weaponry nomenclature and care. Actually the training was pretty interesting and seemed to go by quickly. At the very least it kept us away from Sgt. Thomas.

After our afternoon training sessions, we would be marched or trucked back to the company area and this is when Thomas would harass us. He would find some little thing and turn it into a big thing and have us do extra PT or confine us to the company area. He especially did not like Bob and me. I don't think he liked anyone from Chicago. He was forever throwing shots at us about Chicago and that guys from there were shitbags. He would goad us every chance he got. We never gave him anything but he'd still find something and throw us on a detail. We really despised him and we looked forward to the day that we'd get away from him.

Thomas' assistant, Sgt. Purvis, was a nice guy. He knew Thomas was a jerk and I don't think he had much use for him. Thomas looked down on Purvis because he had not been to Nam. The fact of the matter was that Purvis was a far better soldier. He really knew his stuff and was very helpful in the training sessions. When Thomas wasn't around and Purvis was in charge, everything went very smooth. He just wanted you to do your job and would show you ways to make life easier and it seemed that everyone liked him.

Method of Specialty or MOS training began. My MOS was to be 11C10 or indirect fire crewman. If I was successful and passed the gunners test with the 81mm mortar, I would be assigned to the weapons platoon otherwise I would revert to 11B10 or light weapons platoon.

Sgt. Purvis was an excellent gunner and he took me under his wing and coached me. I think the more Thomas messed with me the more Purvis wanted me to excel. He taught us that the gunner was only as good as his assistant gunner. He teamed me up with a kid from Connecticut by the name of Roderick and we hit it off right away.

Roderick was a real east coaster, very funny and quick witted. He loved to play cards so he and Bob hit it off together also. Roderick was a great card player and so was Bob. They would get a game going in the barracks and one or the other would win. I made out pretty good too as I sort of became the loan man and they would juice me. I don't play cards myself but I loved to watch them as they suckered people in. They would argue about who was the best poker player. It was really a laugh listening to them go on and on about it and never giving an inch.

The mortar training was moving along and we were getting the hang of it. They would rotate us from one job to another and have us break the gun down and carry all the different pieces on marches in order for us to get used to the carry. We had to dig the mortar pits and set the base plate and aiming stakes. Finally the gunner test day came and Roderick and I qualified as experts. This was good because we had a chance that we would be assigned to the mortar platoon of our combat companies if there was an opening.

The next phase of training was survival school. It involved surviving without food, water, and separated movement at night and during the day. Camouflage, silent movement, hand signals, concealment, escape, and evasion were some of the courses that we had. We all knew how important these things were to our survival in Vietnam.

There was an escape and evasion course at Tigerland that was mandatory. Two men had to go through this course undetected at night while the cadre would try to find you. If caught, you got your ass kicked and thrown into a Viet Cong prison and some torture was introduced. The torture was nothing crippling but it was just something you didn't want to go through. Nobody was looking forward to this course except Sgt. Thomas and naturally he was in charge of the prison and torture.

I made Bob laugh when I told him that we should excel at this with our Chicago training of running from the cops or the older guys that we would torment until they came after us. It was quite a thrill as I recall. I told him if that didn't work just to picture us spending the night with Thomas and his asshole friends. I really did believe that I could do well at this because as a kid I was good at escape and evasion. I never got caught or was it just pure luck?

Bob and I prepared for our turn on the course. We used black cloth tape around our biceps, calves, and thighs, and our dog tags for silence. We put camouflage grease on our faces and did our steel pots in vegetation. We were now ready to go.

The course coordinator led us to our starting point and issued us an army flashlight with a red lens, a compass, and a small plastic laminated topigraphical map of our route and destination. Supposedly the enemy patrols did not know our routes and they would be on normal night combat patrol, listening posts, and ambushes.

We got the signal to move out and we were off into the dark Louisiana forest. We were lucky there was a partial moon which would help us see. The down side was there were a lot of dried branches on the ground that could create a noise hazard. We decided that the best course of action was to move slowly and stop and listen occasionally. The course was five miles and we figured that it would take us about three hours to reach our destination. Evasion was the key issue. If we were spotted and chased we could become disoriented and that would be disastrous because neither one of us had much compass experience.

We got off to a good start. We were in a pine forest and we were moving from tree to tree, one at a time, and making sure that we were together. If separated, there was no way that we could call out. We had an emergency plan that if separated, the lead man with the flashlight would shine the red light through his shirt to the rear and hope for the best.

It was unbelievably quiet in the forest. It was almost as if the nocturnal creatures were aware of our presence. Even a breaking twig under foot seemed loud. I was sure that I could hear my heart beating. We were about thirty-five minutes into the course when I thought I saw something. I peered into the blackness and sure enough I saw the glow of a cigarette. This was a cardinal mistake for anyone on patrol to smoke. A cigarette glow can be seen from a good distance. Bob and I quickly took cover in the brush. We put a little distance between us and waited. As the patrol came closer, they were much louder. There were at least ten men all dressed in black. They were communicating verbally so it was easy to track them. The patrol passed us and we gave them a little extra time just to make sure. I took a time check and motioned to Bob and we were on our way.

Another hour passed and according to my calculations we were right on course. We came upon a clearing and we knew this spelled trouble. There was an old armor trail across the clearing and it just seemed too easy so we opted to skirt around the clearing. It would take a little longer but we both thought it best. We worked our way around the clearing and just as we got around it, all hell broke loose. Blank rounds were being fired and there was lots of screaming. I guessed that the team behind us had been spotted and was being pursued. We froze in our position until everything was quiet and then we began again and trying very hard to be low profiled and quiet.

A light rain began to fall and I knew that would be helpful because the patrol cadre wouldn't want to get soaked and would probably seek cover. We kept plodding along maintaining a little quicker pace. The rain was now very steady and made things miserable and slippery. We were descending down into a little ravine and I thought it would be a good place to check our map and progress. I knew we were getting close to our destination. Up the other side of the ravine and approximately a half mile and we would be there.

There would be a defense perimeter and we would have to use the proper procedure and identification in order to cross the friendly lines. We did this successfully and were greeted by other successful teams and a nice cup of hot coffee inside a GP tent.

Bob looked at me and said, "And I thought you couldn't read. You really didn't do too bad for a guy from Brainerd."

We found out at the end of the exercise that about ten teams had been captured and imprisoned with our good buddy Thomas.

We could only imagine what it would have been like for us if he'd got his hands on us. The friendly cadre loaded us onto a deuce and half and drove us to our company area. We looked like drowned rats and we were filthy dirty. All we wanted to do was get the clothes off and hit the showers and try to get a little rest. We were just out of the shower when the door of the barracks burst open and Thomas came storming in and started bitching about us tracking up the floor and that no one was going to rest until it was cleaned.

That's just what you needed to hear after a night in the rain and the bush. We got the mop and bucket out and started cleaning and mumbling.

Thomas strode up to Bob and I, in his usual cocky manner, and said, "How did you two duds make it thu that course? Musta paid somebody. I know you ain't smart 'nuf to make it. You got more luck than sense. Both of ya are the sorriest asses I ever saw. Can't wait to get ya outta here. You get to Nam and you'll be in a body bag in a month if ya make it that long."

One thing about this guy is that you learned to keep your mouth shut no matter what he said. I would have loved to tell him that he was the main reason that we made it.

We were now at the end of our training so it would soon be time to say goodbye to Ft. Polk, Tigerland, and most of all our dear friend, Sgt. Thomas. As miserable as it was, I really felt that I was in great physical condition that I had learned a lot. I even made soldier of the week the last week of training and I'm sure Thomas didn't like that but it really felt like a little payback for me. I couldn't help but wonder what could make a guy act like that. If you took the Army from him, he'd be a nobody. I also felt that if a jerk like him could make it back from Nam so could I.

Two days passed and we were all promoted to private E2 which is automatic upon successful completion of advanced training. We were given our orders. True to my premonition, I was assigned to the Republic of Vietnam in the 1st Air Cavalry as an 11C10 infantry indirect fire crewman. Roderick, Hunt, and Wnek were the same and Bob and Ed Metz were assigned to the 25th Infantry Division. Like the Colonel had said at the beginning of our training, half to the Cavalry and the other half to the 25th Division.

We would be going on a thirty day leave and then reporting to Travis AFB, Oakland, California for debarkation to Vietnam.

We made arrangements for our departure on Friday only this time we would take a bus from post to Shreveport and try for a military standby to O'Hare. This would save us a lot of time and money and we'd have more to spend at home. This time, at least, we would get travel pay.

We were excited and happy to pack our duffel bags and clear post. This was the last that we would see of Ft. Polk and it could'nt come soon enough. It had been a tough nine weeks and we were all very anxious to get home and have some fun.

We took an Army shuttle bus to the Greyhound bus depot. I enjoyed that short ride, looking out the window, watching Ft. Polk fade into the distance, never to be seen again.

Bob and I decided to grab a cab when we arrived at O'Hare. That would save a lot of time and we'd have more time on Friday night and get our leave time off to a good start.

CHAPTER 4

The Countdown

Everyone was all smiles as we hopped on the Greyhound bus that would carry us to Shreveport. We were all on the same page as to what we were going to do on leave. We were determined to have a good time and make up for the Tigerland experience and the dark cloud that loomed ahead of us.

As the bus rolled through the gates of North Ft. Polk, I knew that I'd never see this place again and that was soon enough. We rolled down the main road to Leesville and turned north on Highway 177. It was a bright sunny August day and probably another Louisiana scorcher but this time we had air conditioning.

Louisiana is called "the sportsman's paradise" and I can see why. There's a lot of water, swamp, and forest so if you hunt and fish, this is the place to be. It is kind of ironic that we were here to learn how to hunt but for a different prey.

Before long we were on the ramp for north Interstate 49 which would take us to Shreveport Airport and home. It was a nice leisurely ride and we were all hopping from seat to seat swapping stories and plans for our leave time. I think we all needed this little trip to relieve all the stress of the past nine weeks. The nice part about it was that no one brought up Vietnam and our individual assignments. It was as if we were all in a bit of denial.

We arrived at the airport in about two and half hours and all we would need is the flight to O'Hare.

We got to the information desk and the attendant said, "Any of you boys headin' for Chicago or New York?"

"You betcha," was the instant response.

He looked up at us and said, "How many of y'all for Chicago?"

He did a quick head count and did the same for New York and said, "Good news for you boys. I got two military C130s gonna be leavin' from the military terminal down yonder and if ya' don't mind roughin' it, the price is right. They can take both groups with no problem but the cargo area of a C130 just has cloth jump seats and it's mighty noisy. I don't suppose that'll bother y'all none!"

He directed us down the main terminal hallway to the military terminal which was all the way at the end.

This was great news, a free ride to O'Hare. Who cares about the amenities of a commercial flight when we could have the extra bucks for leave. It was only a two and a half hour flight and we'd gain an hour in the deal. We grabbed our duffel bags and went down the hall to the military section and there was an Air Force Master Sergeant standing there with a grin on his face.

He said, "We been waitin' for ya'll. We were supposed to be in the air fifteen minutes ago but we got word from the info desk that there'd be a bunch of y'all headin' for O'Hare. No matter though, cuz we're just dead headin' anyhow. All of ya that'r headin' for Chicago, follow me and I'll getcha loaded and we'll get goin'."

We followed him out the door and onto the tarmac and we saw the plane sitting there with its tailgate down which is also the planes cargo ramp. We followed the Sergeant up the ramp and into the plane. He directed us where to stack our bags and pointed to the jump seats along both sides of the plane. There were fifteen of us so it didn't take long for him to log us in and get us and our bags strapped in.

He gave us a little history and nomenclature of the C130. He told us that the C130 is the workhorse of the U.S. military. It is a multifunction deployment plane for troops and cargo and is used by the airborne troops for their air assault jumps. Just then, a red light came on and he walked to the back of the plane and pushed on a lever that activated the hydraulics that lifted and closed the tailgate. He secured it and then seated himself and

strapped on his seat belt.

He shouted loud enough for all to hear, "We're gonna take off now so check your belts."

This was my first flight on a C130 and little did I know that there would be many more. As a matter of fact, this was only the fourth flight of my life and the other three were related to coming and going in the Army. There are no windows in the cargo hold of the C130 and it's dimly lit so you really do feel like cargo.

We felt the plane start to move and we knew that we were on our way. The plane came to a stop and we heard the roar of the turbo prop engines as the pilot revved for take off. When he released the brakes, we lurched into each other and toward the back of the plane as it accelerated for take off. Soon we were airborne and the sergeant was out of his seat.

He shouted to us, "You boys can loosen your seatbelts but I'd like y'all to keep them on and remain seated durin' the flight as we might hit a lil' turbulence and if you're standin' you might take a bad fall. I'm used to the motion of the plane so I can move about. I'll be checking on y'all now and then so if there's a problem let me know." He went forward through the cockpit door and shut it behind him.

Bob Olejniczak was sitting beside me. We exchanged a few words but soon found out that conversation was annoying with all the noise. It would be a boring trip and not the most comfortable, but just the time saved made it well worth while. Every half hour or so, the master sergeant came back in cargo to check on us and to good naturedly heckle us for not being smart enough to join the Air Force. Little did he know, we all agreed with him. Anything would be better than combat infantry in Vietnam!

The red light popped on and the Sergeant came into the cargo hold and announced, "Okay boys, it's the moment y'all been waitin' for. We are gonna start our descent and approach for landing, so cinch up them seatbelts and get ready for touchdown."

I could feel the plane descending and as usual I felt the pressure in my ears. I felt the rear wheels make contact and the nose of the plane dropped down and the pilot began his slowdown and we all lurched toward the front of the plane. Soon we were taxiing toward the military section of O'Hare.

The pilot came over the speaker system and said, "This is Major Bill Courtney and on behalf of myself and my crew I would like to wish all of you young men the very best on your leave time and on your Vietnam tour. I'm headed that way myself so maybe our paths will cross again. Good luck!"

The Sergeant hit the tailgate lever and it slowly descended and touched the tarmac. We grabbed our duffel bags and made our way down the ramp and on into the terminal. This was the greatest, no time lost waiting for baggage and best of all, it was free!

Bob and I said our goodbyes to the other guys and hailed a cab. It was sure great to see Chicago streets again and in less than an hour I would be home. We drove down the Kennedy Expressway and it was a beautiful sight to see the downtown skyline on the horizon. Chicago really is a beautiful city and it never looked better to me than it did right now. We passed through Hubbard's Cave and the downtown area and onto the Dan Ryan Expressway and on to the 87th Street Exit. It was a short ride west to Bob's house in Gresham and less than a mile to my own. We said our goodbyes and I told Bob that I'd see him in Oakland. He had a little different plan for going to Oakland so we wouldn't be making the trip together this time.

It was about 7:00 by the time the cab rolled up in front of my house and as usual my mother, my aunt Helen, and neighbors, Sue and Bill, were sitting out in the front on lawn chairs and enjoying a beautiful summer evening. That's one thing that I always loved about Chicago city life was that everyone enjoyed being outside and talking to each other. Of course no one had central air conditioning at that time so that was also a real good reason to be outside.

I paid the cabbie my share of the fare and walked into a whole bunch of hugs, kisses, and handshakes. I could see the pride in my mother's eyes as she looked me up and down in my summer class

A uniform. My brother Jack came out and greeted me and told me that my Pontiac convertible was in the garage and that he had been starting it for me and it had a full tank of gas.

I went into the house and headed for my room. I stretched out on my bed and felt the comfort that I'd been missing for weeks. Army bunks are a three inch mattress on a flat bed of springs and when you lie down on it, it wraps around you and you really can't move so this was pure heaven to be in a real bed. I could smell the detergent that my mom used when she washed the bedding. One thing that I had learned in the Army was how much I loved my home.

I looked around the room and I was flooded with memories. This had been my grandfather's room. I can still picture it the way it was when he was alive. I could picture all his furniture and how it was arranged. I had redone the room about two years before going in the Army and it was the nicest room in the house. Everything was new and nice and that made it seem even more comfortable. I could just imagine what it would be like in thirty short days.

I picked up the phone and started calling all my buddies to tell them I'd be home for the next month and we all decided to meet up at the Beverly Lounge and have a few drinks. The Beverly Lounge was one of our favorite haunts. It was very plush inside and they usually had some decent entertainment and a dance floor. There were always some nice looking chicks hanging out in there on the weekends. There was also a good restaurant right next door and the Beverly Drive-in for coffee later on. I knew lots of people in this area, so hooking up was never a problem. Friday night was usually the best night to be out on the hunt.

I got dressed in some nice civilian clothes and splashed on some after shave cologne and made my way down to my neighbor's garage where my car was stored. It was a beautiful night so I put the top down and pulled my Pontiac out onto the street and turned on the radio to some good sounds. This was the way that it should be; the wind in my hair and feeling good about the night. I turned onto Ashland Avenue and stepped on the gas and felt the response from the 389 engine. I listened to the deep roar of the dual exhaust as the car accelerated and in a few minutes, I was there.

I walked into the lounge and my friends, Jim Kearney and Jim Layton, were sitting at the bar waiting for me. We ordered a round of drinks and I threw a ten dollar bill on the bar and Jim Layton picked it up and handed it back to me and looked at Al the bartender and owner.

Jim said, "His money's no good in here. His drinks are on us."

Al reached across the bar and shook hands with me and said, "This one's on me, Bobby!"

Jim Kearney looked at me with his devilish smile and said, "Rube, did you see the moth fly out of that Lugan's wallet."

"Very funny asshole, you've still got the money from your baptism" replied Jim Layton.

With those digs, they were off and running. These two could go at each other all night and never get mad. I had known these guys from my earliest days and I was used to their banter.

More and more people that I knew kept coming in and it was like old home week. It seemed like I just got there and the bartender was giving the last call for a drink at closing time. We went outside to my car and talked for another hour before we called it a night.

I woke up the next day at ten o'clock and my mother and my Aunt Helen were in the kitchen waiting to cook me a special breakfast. I sat down at the kitchen table and had a home cooked breakfast of bacon and eggs, fruit, toast and coffee. The kitchen had always been the hub of our house. It seems that everyone including guests always migrated into the kitchen and my mother was right there to make them feel at home. I can't begin to say how many of my friends were fed in that kitchen and this day was no exception.

My mother's two brothers, Pat and John walked in and sat down with me. They were my heroes. After my father passed away twelve years earlier, they were always there for us. They were the biggest lesson in family loyalty that I would ever learn. They knew what I would be facing and they had been through the same thing five decades before. It may not have been the exact same scenario but the reality was. I tried to be as optimistic as possible and to let them know that some way I would get through this thing.

On the brighter side there was Kathleen. She was the breath of fresh air that I needed. She had shoulder length dark hair and was very petite and her smile and laugh were addictive. When she wanted something she went after it with everything she had. She had a quick wit and knew how to use it to flirt. Even though she was four years younger than me, she managed to get my attention. I was very used to dating girls older than myself but she was able to change that easily enough. She loved to tease but she also had a knack for knowing when not to. She was very passionate and loved long make out sessions and that's when she was in the driver's seat. She knew what a man wanted and how to control it. I would spend all of my dating time with her and enjoy every minute. She gave me a send off that I would never forget.

Time once again was flying by. It seems like whenever you are having a great time with family, friends, and lover that there isn't enough time to say and do all the things that you want to or need to. Thirty days sounds like a long time but I found out just how short it really is. I also found out how many people cared about me and at a later date it would become my cornerstone in Vietnam. I would understand where internal strength comes from. It was something that I had never thought about before. It was the something that later would keep me going.

I was looking at my last week before leaving for Oakland and my mother told me that she was having a party for me on the Saturday before my departure and asked me who of my friends that I would like to be there along with the family and neighbors. I suggested that we make it a "stop by and say goodbye party" rather than a big party that would go on for hours. People could come and go and her house could accommodate that much better. I tried not to think about it too much because I knew that it could be an emotional time seeing everyone under those circumstances. My mother and brother handled all the arrangements and I continued to make the best of my last week.

The last Friday of my leave, I had a date with Kathleen and I thought maybe a nice dinner and long talk would be nice. It would give me a chance to tell her how much that she had meant to me and maybe even make a few plans for the future. She had been staying with her grandparents who lived just three blocks north on the same street. That also made things nice for me because she was so close.

I got dressed and jumped in my car and headed for Kathleen's grandparents two flat. I walked up to the first floor and knocked on the door. I heard Kathleen's grandpa, Ted, call out to me, "Come on in, Bob. The door's open." I walked in and there was Ted in his easy chair watching television. I shook hands with him and made small talk. I had known Ted and his wife, Mabel, most of my life. They were from my old neighborhood in Park Manor and had been insurance customers of my dad.

A few minutes later Kathleen came into the living room and she was looking really good. She had also dressed for the occasion.

She looked at me and smiled and said, "Before we go can you go down in the basement and take a quick look at the cord on my grandpa's table saw? It's a little frayed and he just wants to know if it's okay."

Ted looked up at me and nodded his head, "I'd appreciate it, Bob."

I said that I would and we headed down the stairs and into the basement. It was dark and Kathleen was pulling on my arm and I wondered what she was up to.

I said, "Where's the light switch?"

"Some kind of electrician you are. Can't even find the light switch. I'm not letting you fix my shorts," she said coyly.

"Wanna bet," I said.

At that very moment the lights came on and there was about thirty people screaming, "Surprise!!!" I was really blown away.

I looked at Kathleen and said, "You really got me this time but I'll get you later."

She replied, "Oh you think so. Think ya' can handle it?"

She had invited my closest friends and some of her family, all of whom I knew very well. I was so impressed at how she had put this together without me finding out. It was really a nice party and we all had a great time. The party lasted until about one and then people began to say their goodbyes and before long we were alone.

I looked into her eyes and said, "Kathleen, I think this was the nicest thing that anyone has ever done for me. I never expected this."

She said, "Jimmy and I have been planning this for quite a while. You know what you mean to him and he's very worried about you. He won't say anything. You know how he is and I wanted to show you what you have meant to me as well." I grabbed her hand and led her over to the couch.

I said, "I've got a promise to keep."

What a night, I was feeling totally happy as I made my way to my ragtop and drove home. A convertible was the car for me. There is something about the openness, a feeling of freedom that I love to this day. In the sixties, a sharp car was the thing. Saturday morning would be the time to get the wheels shining for date night. The neighbors would be teasing me about wearing the paint off. My friends would roll up to find out what was up and share a little guy talk.

My mother, aunt, and brother were busy preparing for my goodbye party. My mother had it set up with everyone that the party would be 3 to 10pm and come when you want. It was going to be a nice easy way to say goodbye. I got showered and dressed and people started to arrive. I couldn't believe the number of people coming and going. My family, friends, and neighbors just kept streaming in.

Kathleen and her cousin Kathleen came about seven and they were dressed to the nines. They had white dresses on and they both looked beautiful. Everyone thought that they were twins. They both had long dark hair and big blue eyes that were glistening with mischief. Kathleen's cousin was dating a Marine and she loved to tell me that the Marine Corps was the only branch of the service. I think her boyfriend convinced her that Marines were invincible. Soon we would both find out how invincible we were. I had to apologize to the girls for not being able to spend more time with them but there were just so many people.

I spotted my cousin, Jean and her family, coming through the door and I was shocked to see that her husband, Bernie, was with them. Bernie wasn't big on family parties and usually found an excuse not to attend. He was a quiet man and I suppose it was boring for him. I knew that he was a WWII vet and that he had landed on Utah beach on D Day. He was in the 4th Infantry Division and had been part of Gen. Patton's push through France and on into Germany. I'm sure that he saw a lot of combat but he never spoke about it.

Bernie came over to me and shook my hand and said, "You know you're in trouble don't you?"

I acknowledged.

He said, "The only advice I have for you is; don't be a hero. Keep focused all the time and do your job. Every time I look at the paper all I see is the 1st Cavalry. They are the airmobile strike force and with those helicopters they will be dropping you into harms way any time they spot a sizable force. Do you get what I'm trying to say? We all want you back here in one piece."

I thanked him for his concern and told him that I would follow his advice. That was the most that Bernie ever had to say to me but I knew that it came from the heart and I thanked him for coming.

He said, "I had to come and tell you that."

At that point, I knew my family was very worried about me and how serious the situation was. They knew that this might be the last time they ever saw me.

The party started to taper off by 9:30 and I directed some attention toward Kathleen. She looked very sad and we both knew that our time was growing short.

She looked at me with serious eyes which I hadn't seen before and said, "I know that you are going to make it back home. I can feel it. You just do what you gotta do and it will happen."

I told her that she could count on that and I asked her to write to me and that would be a big help. She said that she would write and that she and Kathleen had to get going. I walked them outside and put my arms around Kathleen and gave her a passionate kiss. It would be a long time before we could do that again so we made it good. Kathleen's brother and my buddy, Jim, came out and we shook hands and he handed me a package.

He said, "There's a 380 automatic in there and some ammo. Keep it with you just in case. Don't do anything stupid. Okay?"

We were all starting to get a little emotional so we said our goodbyes and the three of them jumped into Jim's Olds Starfire and they were gone.

I went back into the house and started to help with the cleanup which was already under way. My mother looked at me with tears in her eyes.

She said, "What time do we have to leave tomorrow to get you to the airport, Bob?"

I responded, "I probably should be there no later than 2 o'clock so Jack and I will have to leave by 1:15 or so."

She looked me in the eyes and said, "I'm going too?"

"No, mom, I don't want you to go. I want to say goodbye to you right here in our home and I'll want to say hi right here as well when I come home. It is going to be very hard for all of us to say goodbye and I know that it is best to do it right here."

I knew that she didn't like it but I knew that it had to be.

The next morning I was up at 9 o'clock and did my packing. I was going to wear civilian clothes to San Francisco. I planned on getting a room for the night and spending my last stateside night in the downtown area. Monday morning I would catch a bus to Travis AFB in Oakland which was the Army's replacement depot for Nam. I went into the kitchen and my mom was preparing a light lunch for us. I could see that she was crying even though she was doing her best to hide it.

I said to her, "Mom, I'm gonna be back. With all your prayers and everyone else's, I can't miss. A year goes by fast and before you know it I'll be back."

She didn't turn around but just nodded her head. We made small talk while we ate and tried to stay away from the Vietnam topic.

Time flew by that morning and before I knew it, it was time for me to go. There were lots of hugs and kisses. I felt so sorry for my mom. It was so hard for her. There really are no words that would describe that moment when I went out the door. My next door neighbors, Bill and Sue Kerwin, were waiting for me outside and they were both teary eyed. They were more than just neighbors, they were like family. That was another thing that I always loved about the neighborhood; it was filled with good and caring people. I gave my brother a wink and we threw my bags in the trunk and we were off to O'Hare.

It was only about a thirty-five minute run to the airport and we parked the car in the airport garage so that Jack could stay with me until boarding time. He could also stay to watch the plane taxi to the runway. He told me that he would write and let me know how everything was going at home and I said the same.

I said to him, "Take care of Mom and Aunt Helen and I'll do the best I can and the rest is up to the Creator. Who knows, maybe this war will come to an end before long."

The flight attendant started to call for boarding for my flight so we shook hands and he wished me luck. I could tell he was feeling very emotional and so was I. We said our goodbyes and I boarded the 737 for San Francisco. I took my seat by the window and I could see Jack standing by the gate window and he was wiping his eyes with a handkerchief. I had a very hollow and empty feeling as the plane started to move and taxi toward the runway. I just stared out that window and wondered what was in store for me.

CHAPTER 5

Debarkation

The plane roared down the runway and I could feel the wheels leaving mother earth and within two minutes I could see O'Hare below and my last look at Chicago for a year. We climbed to our cruising altitude and the smoking light came on. After all the emotional turmoil of the day, I couldn't wait to light up one of my Lucky Strikes. I introduced myself to the fellow seated next to me and he did the same. He was Fr. Tom Morrison, a Catholic priest, from San Jose, California. He had just spent a week with his family in Bellwood, Illinois. I told him that I was en route to Vietnam and the 1st Cavalry via Travis AFB. He told me that his younger brother was in Vietnam with the 1st Division and that he would be coming home at Thanksgiving.

Fr. Morrison was a very easy person to talk to and we talked the whole flight and he managed to take my mind off my destination. He was very familiar with San Francisco and he suggested that I stay at the Balmoral Hotel on Clay Street. He said that it was a nice quiet clean place and quite reasonable and that there were lots of good places to eat in the area. I was really glad that I had a priest sitting next to me on the flight. I'm not a real religious guy but I considered it a good omen and he seemed to have just the right conversation for someone in my position.

The seat belt and no smoking lights came on and the Captain announced that we would be starting our approach and that we'd be on the ground in approximately fifteen minutes. He gave us a brief weather rundown and the standard - Thank you for flying United Airlines. While we were taxiing into the terminal area, Fr. Morrison asked me if he could give me a lift to the hotel as one of the parish priests would be picking him up. He said that it would be no bother and that he could point out the bus terminal which was within walking distance of the hotel.

He said, "It's the very least that I could do for one of our nation's defenders. It's too bad you don't have a little more time, Bob. I could show you around a bit."

I thanked him for his kindness and told him that I would really appreciate the ride. We went to baggage and grabbed our luggage and walked out the arrival doors and our ride was waiting for us. An older gentleman stepped from the driver's seat of a gorgeous new black Olds 98 sedan and walked up and greeted Fr. Morrison.

"Welcome home father and who is this young fellow?"

Fr. Morrison replied, "This is Pfc. Bob Powers from Chicago and he is en route to Vietnam via Travis. I told him we'd give him a lift to the Balmoral Hotel and point out the bus terminal. I also want to make sure that he gets a room or we'll take him back to the rectory with us. Bob, this is Fr. Bill Doyle my fellow priest and pastor from St. Mary's in San Jose. Father was a chaplain in the Korean War."

Fr. Bill was a slight built man with graying black hair and big smile that put you at ease right away. We got into the car and Fr. Tom got behind the wheel and looked back at me.

"My parents bought me this car for me last year when I was transferred out here from the Chicago. I drove it from Chicago and it was like riding on a cloud. I really missed this car when I went home but I'm sure Fr. Bill enjoyed it while I was gone, right father?"

It was 6 o'clock when we rolled up in front of the Balmoral Hotel. It was a beautiful sunny afternoon. I got out of the car and said goodbye to Fr. Bill and he told me to stop by St. Mary's on the way home in a year and he and Fr. Tom would show me the good side of the Bay area. I told him that I'd make a point of it and thanked him for his hospitality.

Fr. Tom opened the trunk and I muscled my duffel bag up onto my shoulder and we headed into the hotel lobby. Fr. Tom strolled up to the desk and the clerk looked up from his newspaper.

"Hey, Fr. Tom, what brings you downtown?"

"I brought you some business, Charlie, and I expect the same from you this Sunday," he said jokingly. "This is my friend, Bob, from Chicago and he needs a room for the night and your great advice on eateries in the area and also where not to go. We've got to keep this lad from all the dens of iniquity. Uncle Sam expects to see him at Oakland in the morning."

"No problem father, consider it done," he chuckled.

Fr. Tom and I shook hands and I thanked him for all his help. He gave me his blessing.

"Bob, the best of luck to you and come home safely and may God be with you!"

He turned and walked toward the door and then looked back at Charlie.

"Charlie, you know the address at St. Mary's and you'll direct it to my attention," and he was gone.

Charlie had me sign in and gave me a key for room 711 and pointed toward the elevator.

I had my wallet in my hand and I said to Charlie, "I'll be checking out early tomorrow so what do I owe you?"

He laughed and said, "Fr. Tom took care of it. He is one helluva guy. I'll tell you, Bob, he makes St. Mary's. It was the best thing that ever happened to the parish when he came from Chicago and partnered up with Fr. Doyle. They make a great team! Do you know him a long time?"

I was speechless and told Charlie, "I just met him today on the flight from Chicago!"

"See what I mean; what a guy. He'd give you the shirt right off his back. Well, you probably want to bring your bag upstairs and freshen up so I'll let you go. You're in room 711 and it's the first door on your left as you get off the elevator. Stop by on your way out and I'll give you the do's and don'ts."

I found room 711 and went in. 711 were the last three digits of my service number and another numerical coincidence. These sevens and ones keep appearing. How strange! There was nothing fancy about the room but like the good father had said, it was clean and comfortable. The furnishings were old and kind of home-like in a way. I flopped on the bed and closed my eyes and tried to put the days' events in order before doing a nice shower and going out for something to eat.

After a refreshing little snooze, I picked myself up and hit the shower. It felt great to have the cool water running over me. It was just what I needed to perk me up. I got dressed and went down to the lobby desk. Charlie was sitting behind the desk reading a newspaper.

I said to him, "I'm starving, Charlie, send me to some place good. It may well be my last shot at a good meal and a few drinks."

Charlie recommended an Italian restaurant about two blocks away and I couldn't get there fast enough. The restaurant was very nice and had a nice Tuscan ambiance. I ordered a carafe of Italian red wine with my chicken cacciatore. The meal was exceptional. The only part of it that I didn't enjoy was being alone. I absolutely hate eating alone; I find myself eating too fast so that I can leave. I have to tell myself to slow down and enjoy. I finished up and paid the bill and went out into a beautiful San Francisco evening.

The next question was: what do I do now? Maybe I should find a nice bar and have a couple drinks. That didn't appeal to me and it might make me melancholy. I decided to go for a walk and do a bit of sightseeing. I walked around for about an hour and I just couldn't seem to get into it. No matter how I tried, my mind would just revert back to tomorrow. I decided to go back to my room and get a good nights' sleep.

I went back to the hotel, took a hot shower and went to bed. The good nights' sleep that I planned on wasn't going to happen either. It was a toss and turn night with very little sleep. I probably should have had a couple of drink; it might have knocked me out. I'm the type of person, the unknown bothers. I guess it's because of my home life. Everything was always very secure and predetermined. I wondered what tomorrow would be like.

I was up at the first light and I got dressed in my Class A uniform and headed down to the desk to check out. Charlie wasn't around so I told the night manager to thank him for me and I was on my way. I shouldered my duffel bag and made my way to the bus depot. There was a bus right out in front of the depot that was marked U.S. Army Processing Facility, Oakland. The driver waived me over.

"Goin' to Nam via Oakland? I nodded and he pointed at the storage compartment and said,

"Toss your bag in there and grab yourself a seat. We'll be leaving when we're full up."

I climbed up the steps into the bus and I heard a voice ring out.

"Hey, hot shot, over here!"

There was Bob Olejniczak sitting three rows back with his usual ball busting grin.

"I thought you'd be in Canada by now," I replied.

"Are you kidding? I wouldn't miss this ride for the world. You know see the world and all that bullshit. How bad can it be? At least, we're gettin' away from that asshole Thomas.

That's something I liked about Bob, he was always trying to make like none of this bothered him. Just put the blinders on and keep on moving and it worked. He was really a tough guy. There was no way he'd let anyone know that this wasn't easy.

It was only about a half hour ride across the bay to Oakland and then the fun began. This was typical of the Army, hurry up and wait, lines for this and lines for that. Eventually we were herded into a huge airplane hanger. There were a bunch of bunks with just mattresses so we each grabbed one and sat down. An Army sergeant came in and told us that we would be deploying for Vietnam within twenty-four hours and that the only time that we could leave the hangar was when we were taken to the mess hall to eat. There were guards on the doors so we knew that they meant it. Actually the only thing that we were waiting for was a full plane load but they didn't tell us that. We had nothing to read and it was

very noisy so there wouldn't be any napping while we waited.
Before too long, we found more of our Ft. Polk comrades and we
all sat around talking about all the fun that we had on leave. There
were some great and funny stories to help pass the time and no one
talked about Nam.

We were only about two hours into our storage when we were
told to line up single file. We were given our orders and the hangar
door was opened. We saw a commercial Flying Tiger Airline jet sitting on the tarmac and two rows of MPs with side arms stretching
from the hangar door to the steps going up into the plane. I found
that to be very demeaning. What did they think, we'd change our
minds? I think if that was the case, we wouldn't have shown up. We
walked the gauntlet to the plane, climbed the stairs and took a seat.

Bob whispered, "The Army sure knows how to make you feel
good. I ain't felt this good since the last time I got my ass kicked.

As soon as we were all boarded, the plane taxied to the runway and we were on our way. This was a thirteen hour flight from
Travis AFB to Ton Son Nhut Airport in Saigon. It is a long flight
but when you're headed for Vietnam, it's very short.

The Captain came over the PA system and said, "We'll be
starting our descent soon and we will be turning all lights off at a
few thousand feet for the obvious reason. Do not be alarmed, this
is standard procedure for night landings. Good luck to you all on
your tour."

It was about 1:30 am Vietnam time when we touched down.
We were bussed to a temporary repo depot at Bien Hoa. A short
nap in an open sided tent and we were awakened in the dark by the
sound of jet fighters screaming down the runway with orange and
blue flames shooting from their afterburners. It was quite a sight to
see fighter after fighter take off and join a formation and head out
on a sortie. We didn't know it at the time that Bien Hoa was a huge
airbase for fighter bombers.

As soon as it was light, we were transported to Long Binh
which was the main replacement depot for Army personnel. Long
Binh was a terrible place. It reminded me of a concentration camp.
The tents were open sided and bunks with just mattresses, lousy
food, and in general everyone seemed to have a real bad attitude.

We were told that we'd be there for about three days while our assignments and orders were cut. The place was hot and dusty, the only shade was in the tents. I couldn't wait to get out of there, but I was about to find out that it was going to get a lot worse than this. When I think back, I could have stayed there for my 365 days a whole lot easier and safer than where I was going.

Two days later our orders came through and we were all going different directions. I was assigned to B Company 5th Battalion 7th Cavalry so it was time to say goodbye and good luck to Bob and the guys that I hung around with. I shook hands with Bob and I wished that we could have stayed together. I had so many laughs with him, I knew that I was going to miss him.

Rich Roderick drew the same assignment as me and that eased the pain somewhat. Those of us who were assigned to the 1st Cavalry Division were bused to an airfield and boarded onto a C130 for a short flight to Camp Radcliff, the division base camp at An Khe. There were about forty troops on board. We touched down at the base airstrip, grabbed our duffel bags and off loaded the plane. A sergeant, who was in charge of our group, said that some-one would be along to get us and to assemble along side of the tar-mac and wait. We watched the C130 turn around and take off.

It was raining pretty steady and we were getting soaked. A few minutes later another C130 landed and taxied up near where we were grouped. The tailgate went down and two Air Force crew-men began dragging dead bodies off the plane and lining them up along side the tarmac. The bodies were wrapped in rain ponchos. There were lifeless bloody arms and legs hanging out from the ponchos and the musty stench of the combat infantry permeated the air. It was a shocking and upsetting trip into reality. This was how it was and how it was going to be; this was our introduction to the 1st Cavalry

The sergeant, our unofficial leader, went over to see if he could help and he was talking to the crew and they told him that these KIA's were from the 7th Cavalry. Rich and I were very quiet after hearing this. This was the first time in my life that I had seen anything like this and I'm sure the same was true for Rich. I think that it was at this juncture that I convinced myself that I could not and should not take mental pictures of these horrific scenes. I told myself to just keep going forward, do your job, and hope for the best.

We stood in the rain in silence trying not to look across the tarmac at the fallen soldiers. I wondered who they were and who they might have been if it wasn't for this war. It is times like this when it is very difficult to keep it all together.

A small truck came into view and made its way toward us. It stopped and a soldier stuck his head out the window and said, "Anybody for B Company, 5th of the 7th hop on." Five of us grabbed our bags and climbed up into the truck. The truck pulled away and lumbered down a dirt road. There were huge green tents everywhere as we drove along. We made a turn and came to a stop in front of one of these large tents.

The driver got out and said, "You guys can grab your bags and line up over here and Top will be out in a minute."

Rich and I introduced ourselves to the other three guys that were with us and we made small talk about where we were from and where we had previously been stationed. One of the guys, Steve Day, had been in the Army for over a year and had been involved in the Dominican Republic Action with the 82nd Airborne. He told us that his brother was here in the 1st Cavalry with the 77th Field Artillery and that he was looking forward to seeing him. Steve was making a career of the Army and I could tell that he liked the idea of being in Vietnam where the action and rank was. Bill Gould was from New York City, Johnnie Gatlin was from Missouri. Four of us were draftees and most definitely weren't looking for action or a career.

A short slim man in his forties approached us with a clipboard in his hand. He eyed us up and down while chewing on an unlit cigar.

"I'm 1st Sergeant Hare. You can call me Top. Welcome to B Company. Our battalion arrived here last month and presently we are securing Highway 19 but we are supposed to go out in the field in a couple of days." Glancing down at his clipboard, he continued, "Powers and Roderick to the fourth platoon, Day and Gould to the second platoon, and Gatlin to the third platoon. Tomorrow you will

DEBARKATION

begin your in country division training which is for three days. When that is completed, you will join your platoons. These tents are lined up in order: command, supply, 1st, 2nd, 3rd, and 4th platoons. Grab an empty bunk and stow your bags in your respective tents. That's the mess tent over there. Go get some lunch and I'll see you afterward."

We dispersed into our tents and found empty bunks and tossed our bags and went over to the mess tent. There were about two dozen new picnic benches inside and a serving line across the front. There were six mermite (insulated) cans sitting up on a long table.

The mess sergeant looked at us and said, "Grab a tray and plate and help yourselves. There's meat in the first can, veggies in two and three, fruit in four, coffee in five, and lemonade in six. That is how we set up the mess line here and in the field. When you guys are done eating, put your plates, hardware, and trays over here. We have a truck bringing lunch out to the highway and I need you guys to load it."

We dug into the food and grabbed a bench and started to eat. I was really surprised, the food was good. When we had our fill, we went outside and helped load the field cans on the truck.

Everyone so far seemed to have a nice laid back attitude. There were no loud orders or condescending attitudes. It was as if we were now part of a team or family. There were no formalities of rank.

I glanced over at the CQ tent and I saw a red and white cavalry guidon with B-5-7 on it and was positioned next to the door of the tent. At that moment, Top came out and called us over.

"I'm glad to see you guys giving a hand to cookie. We all pitch in and do what we have to. When we came here, this was nothing but a barren field. Everything you see here has been done in two weeks. We all busted ass and got it done. We've got a bunch of good guys who will cover each others' backs. This is my third war and I know what it takes to make it."

A short husky staff sergeant came out of the supply tent and Top introduced him to us as Sgt. Moss, B Company's supply sergeant.

"Sgt. Moss will issue you jungle boots, fatigues, web gear, and an M16. You will have to train and qualify with the M16 and you will have booby trap and rappel training as well at division. That's it for now and you can spend the rest of the day learning your way around the company and battalion areas."

The next morning after mess, we were trucked over to the division training area. The first day was spent learning the M16 nomenclature and qualifying with it. The second day was learning how to rappel from a thirty foot tower and day three was booby traps and a little about the Vietnamese people and their customs and culture. We all completed the training with no problem and returned to the company area. We had dinner and we were sitting around afterwards.

Steve Day said, "We're going to the field tomorrow and I heard that the company is out in Bong Son at LZ Topaz. There's been lots of action out there. I think that's where those troopers that we saw at the airstrip were killed." He continued, "You see that guy over there? His name is Stanton and he was a squad leader and disobeyed a direct order from the CO. I hear they might court martial him but in the mean time the Captain sent him back here until he figures out what to do with him. He might be losing some of them stripes."

Rich asked, "What did he do?"

"He was supposed to take a patrol out at night as a listening post at a predetermined location and he was scared so he had the patrol stay along the highway instead of going where he was supposed to and somehow he got caught."

Steve had been in the Army long enough to know how to get all the info and rumors that were out there. In some ways it's a good thing and in others it's bad. I think sometimes you're better off if you don't know too much and at least you're not worrying about things that you can't control.

CHAPTER 6
Operation Thayer I

Dawn broke the next day and it was already hot and humid at 6:00. We had breakfast and Top told Day, Gould, Roderick, and Gatlin to saddle up and that he would be taking them out to the field and that I would be coming out with the dinner log ship. I was to help out around the company area until then. A huey log ship helicopter flew in and Top and the four troopers jumped on. The chopper lifted off and quickly disappeared into the hazy morning sunrise.

The day went by quickly, I did little chores for anyone that needed help. I got to meet several people from Headquarters Company. One fellow, Tom Malone, told me the history of how the unit was formed and how they had all been together from basic training through advanced unit training. The entire battalion had come over to Vietnam by ship. He said it took two weeks by ship and that a lot of the guys had sea sickness. Tom said that it was cramped quarters the entire voyage and not a very pleasant experience. After hearing that story, I felt lucky to have come over by plane. He told me that the 7th Cavalry was General Custer's Cavalry and was known as the Garry Owen Brigade. It was the only brigade in the Army that used its own salutation of "Garry Owen."

Tom told me that my CO was Captain John Hitti and that he was a competent officer and leader. He said that I had an experienced platoon sergeant by the name of Ray Hartje. Hartje was a three war veteran with the 1st Cavalry. It seemed like Tom knew everyone and after talking with him, I felt more at ease. He had a strong Bostonian accent and I enjoyed listening to it. We had dinner in the mess tent together and I thanked him for explaining everything to me.

I got my M16, steel helmet, web gear, poncho and rucksack, and walked toward the helipad. There was a log ship standing on the helipad with the rotors spinning around. The chopper was completely filled with mermite and five gallon water cans. The pilot was waving for me to get on but there was no where to go. The pilot kept waving at me to get on. I thought to myself, what does he want me to do, climb up on top of the cans. Well, that's exactly what he wanted me to do so I climbed up on top of the cans and the chopper lifted off.

This was my first experience with a helicopter flight and I knew nothing about gravity in flight. I looked out of the side opening and we were banking a turn and I thought for sure that me and those cans were going right out the door and down to mother earth. We climbed up to about one thousand feet and I could see the terrain for miles. The plush green rice paddies, the winding sand colored rivers below, and Hon Cong Mountain with the big 1st Cavalry insignia were quite a site.

It was only a fifteen minute flight to LZ Topaz and we were rapidly descending onto the hilltop and I could see all the positions and troops below. The pilot put the chopper down and troops came to both sides and unloaded very quickly. I learned that the choppers had to be unloaded A.S.A.P. because of sniper fire. They were prime targets. I jumped off the huey and grabbed a mail sack on the way.

One of the unloaders was Rich. He grabbed me by the arm.

"Come on, you're in the fourth platoon with me. I'll take you over to Sgt. Hartje."

He walked me up to a slight built man in his late forties and introduced me. The sergeant shook hands with me and asked me where I was from.

He said, "You're gonna to be in Zepeda's squad. Roderick will get you over to him and he'll square you away."

Roderick and I headed over to Sgt. Zepeda and Rich introduced us. Zep as he was called was an olive complexioned guy in his twenties and seemed to have a real easy going demeanor. He was quick to smile and he was a good listener. I took a liking to him right away.

Hon Cong Mountain – Camp Radcliff – An Khe

He said, "For tonight, I'm gonna pair you up with Rich. We're going through a little reorganization but we should have a handle on it by tomorrow night. You guys can build yourselves a hooch over there and this is your field of vision and fire which overlaps the positions on the right and left. Things should be quiet cuz were on a hilltop with good vision and but keep your eyes and ears open and take turns with guard. Two hours on, and two hours off, got it."

He left us and went over to the next position.

I asked Rich, "What's a hooch?"

He explained to me that it's a tent fashioned by snapping two ponchos together and propping it up with a couple sticks.

I said, "It's beautiful tonight so I don't think that we'll need to make a hooch." He agreed and that was our first mistake.

We had a couple hours of daylight so we both started to write some letters with our newest mailing address. I wrote my mom and then Kathleen. I was thinking a lot about her and the great times that we had while I was home. What a change to be stuck here for the next year. There wouldn't be any pretty faces or parties out here in this hell hole. The only thing that we had to look forward to was R&R but that was a long way off. As I wrote, I tried not to be too descriptive about our conditions and what we might be facing. I thought it best to keep my writing as positive as I could.

It was starting to get dark so Rich and I started our guard watches from a perimeter foxhole that he had dug earlier. I went first from 9 to 11pm and Rich tried to grab two hours sleep. I stared out into the darkness and I could see some flickering fire lights coming from a nearby hamlet. I envisioned the VC trying to silently make their way up the hill and pop a grenade in on me before I knew what happened. It was the first night jitters and my mind was filled with bad scenarios. Rich relieved me at 11 and I tried to go to sleep but I was too jumpy.

About midnight, it started to pour down rain. I covered over with my poncho and the rain was beating on it and there was water running under my body. Between the water running under me and the condensation from breathing under the poncho, I was completely soaked top and bottom and miserable on top of that. This went on all night long and neither one of us got much rest let alone sleep. This was how it was going to be and I was just going to have to get used to it. It started to get light out at 5:30 and before long we could hear the whopping sound of a chopper approaching the hilltop. It was a log ship bringing our chow and water.

After eating and filling our canteens with water, Rich and I were given pack boards with four rounds of high explosive 81mm mortar ammo strapped to it. This is what we would have to carry along with our rifles, ammo, grenades, rucksacks, C rations, and steel pots.

We were going to descend down the hill and begin a search and destroy mission in the valley below. By the time we began, the sun was blazing hot and there was no breeze. We made our way down the hill and the company went into a wedge formation with our platoon closing the back of the wedge. We were spread out across the rice paddies and slogging through the filthy water and grey colored sludge that made up the bottom of the paddies. We could not walk on the dikes because sometimes they were booby trapped.

We crossed the rice paddy fields and entered the hamlet without any resistance. We searched for any sign of VC or their supplies. We had an ARVN interpreter with us and he questioned the villagers as we moved through the hamlet.

The villagers seemed to be old men, women, and children. These poor people had nothing, they literally scratched their existence from the earth. I had never seen anything like this. When you come from the U.S. with all its bounties, it's hard to imagine this type of existence. This was right out of the stone age. There was no plumbing, electricity, glass, or furnishings. The buildings of the villages were mostly mud and thatch. Disease and any type of infection was death for these people. Something as simple as an impacted tooth could be fatal. I felt very compassionate toward them. They were just caught up in this mess and so were we. The big difference was that if we survived we would be able to go home after a year and for them the war just went on with no end.

It was the first week of October and our routine remained pretty much the same. We were moving across the Bong Son Plain, slogging through the rice paddies and hamlets by day and digging in at night. We hadn't made any significant contact other than a sniper round here or there. It was as if the enemy was avoiding contact and of course that was fine with me.

Everyday, I was meeting different guys in my platoon. They were interested in Rich and me because we were the first replacements into the platoon. We were the new kids on the block. We were learning how little we knew about being in the field. These guys were mostly from the west and they were no strangers to the outdoors. They were highly trained for over a year and the NCO's were experienced. I was learning how an infantry company operates and who did what. My conception of how it was going to be was so far off the mark, it wasn't even funny.

Being the ammo bearers in the platoon meant that we would be on perimeter guard at night. There would be three men to a perimeter position. We dug our foxhole and took turns on guard through the night. I was usually with Mike Speck, Jim Pitzen, or Rich. Mike was a wiry slim fellow from Colorado. He was a hard working guy and had a nice easy way about him. Jim Pitzen was a blond curly haired kid from northern Minnesota. He was a great guy and loved to talk about fishing and hunting. He was an outdoorsman and lots of help to me. I had never camped, hunted, or anything so this was another reality shock. I was the city boy, being introduced to the great outdoors, the hard way.

Our squad leader, Zep, watched over us and made sure we had things set up right. He kept us up to speed on what was going on. He was a straight shooter and you could believe what he said, he wasn't into rumors and petty bullshit. He had just made sergeant but he had savvy and I was comfortable with him. We all shared the same goals and number one on the list was to get back home in one piece.

On October 4th, A Company made heavy contact with a sizable force and we were air assaulted into a hot landing zone. As our hueys descended into the rice paddies below, the door gunners opened up with their M60 machine guns into the tree line. The chopper hovered at about six feet and we jumped into the rice paddies below. We were instantly stuck half way to our knees in the muck bottom of the paddy. It was extremely hard to move and the scene was chaotic. We were sitting ducks if the enemy had sight of us and I got my first real taste of fear. I was desperately trying to get my legs moving. I heard the sharp crackling of rifle fire and the feeling that came over me was impossible to describe.

We moved toward the tree line and established our platoon and squads. We made our way through the trees to a large clearing and saw the rest of the company already around the perimeter of the clearing. Our Lieutenant told us to dig the guns in and gave us our positions on the perimeter. We could hear automatic fire that sounded very close. The enemy was moving in our direction and we were the blocking force. The 81mm mortars were set and firing. We supplied the gunners with all the ammo that we had and then we took our spots on the line. The sound of automatic gunfire and the sulfur smell of gunpowder and a bluish haze of smoke was everywhere. The cease fire order was given to the mortars and within minutes artillery fire commenced to our front.

Tension was mounting as we waited for the enemy. An hour passed and the plan was to dig in and maintain this position through the night. Our two lead platoons were firing into a village to their front and the artillery fire was being directed in the same direction. Darkness came quickly and the gunfire ceased. We hunkered down for a long night of waiting. The sound of choppers filled the air. A medevac chopper landed inside our perimeter guided in by flashlight and radio. The wounded were quickly loaded on board and the chopper lifted off and disappeared into the darkness.

For me no amount of training could prepare me for the reality of this situation. I had led a sheltered life and I had never seen anything like this. This was our first taste of battle. The silence was eerie as we peered into the blackness to our front. Would we be attacked during the night? How would we do? This is the big test. We were going to find out what we were made of. Until the time comes, no one knows how they will react to fear.

Throughout the night, light flares were dropped which helped us to see our field of fire. The bad news is that your position can be compromised and draw sniper fire. The night remained silent and I was thankful for that.

At first light, Zep came over to our position and told us what had happened. A Company had lost three troopers and our company had two wounded. I didn't know the fallen troopers but Mike and Zep did and I could see that they were upset. It bothered me to hear that three troopers had been killed but I didn't know them on a personal level and as time went by I would understand that it was better when you didn't know them.

Captain Hitti decided to move into the village where the small arms fire had come from. We got into formation and moved toward the village. We were all expecting gunfire to start at any moment. It didn't happen and we entered the village. My platoon was ordered to search the village. We found several dead NVA but their weapons were gone. We destroyed rice caches and anything else that might be of use to the enemy. Our lead platoon had linked with A Company and there was no further contact. A Company was airlifted to the artillery support LZ and C Company took their place.

We spent the next several days slogging through the rice paddies and going from hamlet to hamlet in search of our elusive enemy. The NVA traveled very light and with the VC to guide them, they could easily outdistance us. They had over one year to figure out how the 1st Cavalry operated. Most of their movement was by night. Their battalion and regiment camps were in the tree covered massifs. Some of these fortifications dated back to the French Indochina War. The enemy would come down into the villages and hamlets at night for food and sex and then seek the tree cover of the massifs by day.

The weather was unbearably hot and we had the usual problems with thirst, hygiene, leeches, insects, and snakes. I was beginning to catch on to ways of dealing with these daily problems. When you have no other options, you will adapt. It is hard to describe this life to someone who hasn't lived it. The lack of sleep, the filth, and the physical challenges were almost as bad as the combat. It was bad to think about these things. The best solution was to just take it one day at a time and hope for the best.

Our company was rotated to the artillery support hilltop LZ for a rest. It would be our job to improve fortifications and secure the artillery batteries. This was a good mission, we were up on a hill with a good field of vision and most of the digging had been done. This also meant hot meals twice a day, mail, and 201 packages which contained beer, cigarettes, soap, toothpaste and brushes, candy, shave cream, and razors. We would have the opportunity to clean up a little, write home, and get a little more sleep. I had lots of catching up to do with my letter writing. I had a lot of people writing me. I appreciated every letter and it was a great morale booster. I responded as best I could and tried not to include anything bad.

Kathleen had been writing me about once a week and I looked forward to her letters. I spent a lot of time thinking about her and what a great time we had. I wondered if she'd still be around when I got out of this mess. Thinking of home was what kept me going. I thought a lot about the past and the future. All I knew is that I just had to get through this and back to what I loved. I had been here for one month and the thought of eleven more months seemed like an eternity.

We got two more replacements into the platoon, Jim Haggerty from Grand Rapids, Michigan and Julio Torres from Coamo, Puerto Rico. Haggerty was a burly guy who laughed a lot. He had a jovial easy going way about him. Torres was a quiet nervous guy. They fit right in with our squad and Rich and I were no longer the new kids on the block. We helped them adjust like we had been helped. We passed along some of the lessons that we had learned and their arrival lightened our load.

We went back into the bush and it was day after day of humping up and down hills, crossing rice paddies, and searching villages. There was only sporadic contact and sniper fire. We were on the move every day and sometimes we made two air assaults in a day.

On the 27th of October, Company B lost its first trooper. SP4 Frank Glowiak was killed by fragmentation wounds. I didn't know Frank but I still felt the loss but nothing like Mike and all the original men of the unit .This would mark the beginning of many more casualties.

CHAPTER 7

Operation Thayer II

At the end of October, Operation Thayer II began. We were told that our performance on Operations Thayer I and Irving had been very successful. The 5th Battalion had killed two hundred enemy soldiers and captured thirty-two. The battalion had lost seven troopers and had several wounded.

On November 1st, we were operating in Binh Dinh Province doing the normal search and destroy just north of Phu Cat. It had been just another hot day of pursuit. Intelligence had reports of a sizable NVA force operating in this vicinity and we were checking it out. Sgt. Hung, our ARVN interpreter, was questioning all the villagers while we systematically searched the hamlets. There were no signs of enemy activity. We were preparing to move on to the next hamlet when the battalion radio came to life. Someone had made contact and Capt. Hitti was on the radio. We knew that we'd be moving to wherever the action was.

Two platoons of the 1st Squadron of the 9th Cavalry had been deployed to an area near Hoai Nhon to recon the suspected enemy locations. Contact was made with a battalion sized force and the two platoons were pinned down. They called for reinforcements and a platoon from our A Company was sent to help and they immediately came under heavy fire and were also pinned down. B Company received orders to assemble along Highway 1 for an air assault. The only thing that we were told is that we would be moved into a blocking position.

The choppers came in and landed on the road and the first wave was on their way with Capt. Hitti and the lead platoons. My squad was slotted for the third wave. It was a short distance to Hoai Nhon so it would only be minutes until the choppers returned for the second wave. We would watch the door gunner and crew chief to see if they dismounted to check for damage. This was a way for us to know how hot the LZ was. The choppers returned for the second wave and there were clouds of dust everywhere. They lifted off quickly and headed north. We stood silent and wondered what we were in for. The choppers returned and we jumped on and we were on our way. The hueys stayed low over the treetops so they would be less of a target. We set down on high ground which was known as LZ Susan. Capt. Hitti was organizing the second and third platoons to move out and attack. The first and fourth platoons would be in reserve.

We moved down off the high ground and crossed a rice paddy and encountered sniper fire. We made it across the paddies and onto dry ground. It seemed to be a burial place with terraced mounds and hedgerows. Within minutes there was automatic weapon fire on our right flank. Capt. Hitti immediately made his way in that direction and we were directed to bolster the right flank. There was sniper fire coming from the trees. The enemy had heavy machine guns and bunker complexes. A three sided attack was mounted and the enemy was overrun. As the enemy retreated, forty-three bodies and many weapons were left behind.

After the battle was over, we learned that we had lost seven troopers and had three wounded. 1st Sgt. Hare was killed along with Sgt. Mendenhall and most of his squad. The enemy had been concealed in spider holes dug in the hedgerows and they had vegetation wrapped around their heads and weapons. When Sgt. Mendenhall and his squad approached the hedgerow, the enemy waited until the squad was right on top of them before they opened up. There was no escape.

Capt. Hitti personally flushed out three bunkers and killed several enemy soldiers. He was under fire the whole time and still directed the battle. After the casualties had been evacuated, he directed artillery fire to ring the embattled units throughout the night to prevent further attacks and probes. Later, Capt. Hitti would be awarded the Distinguished Service Cross for his heroism on that day.

The next day, we returned to LZ Susan. Capt. Hitti gathered the company around him and spoke to us about the battle. I will never forget the emotion in his voice and the tears steaming down his face as he talked about each trooper who had been killed. He mentioned each one by name as he spoke of their sacrifice and courage. This was a painful thing for him as their commander and for the surviving troopers that knew these brave men so well.

Our company secured LZ Susan and we remained there for about a week while our sister companies swept the area for remnants of the 93rd NVA Battalion and the 2nd Viet Cong Regiment that might still be in the area. This was a little time for the guys to sort things out and try and put the horror of the battle behind them. I know that seems like an over simplification but it is the reality of it. We had been in the bush for forty-five days and brigade decided to send the battalion back to An Khe for a short rest and clean-up.

When we arrived back at base camp, we were issued new jungle fatigues and boots. We all got a warm shower and a shave. It was like heaven to be clean again. Battalion supply passed out ice cold beer. I never tasted anything so good. It is amazing how some little things like that can raise your morale.

We spent the next few days cleaning our weapons, writing letters, and getting some precious sleep. No patrols or guard and three hot meals a day, it was like heaven. I bought two cameras from the division post exchange. One of the cameras was a tiny Minolta 16mm. that I could take to the field. The film cartridge was very small and I figured that I could put it in the mail with no problem. I took some nice pictures of the guys and familiarized myself with the cameras. I put the film in the mail and hoped for the best. About half of the film would make it home.

Zep told the squad that we could go into the town of An Khe if we wanted. He gave us a brief rundown of the rules for the

daytime pass. In order to get the pass, a condom had to be purchased. The disease rate from the local prostitutes was very high
and there were some strains of STD's that were incurable. I decided
to go so I hooked up with Rich, Mike, and Jim.

Vietnamese hookers

We caught a military bus from base camp to the town. As
soon as we stepped off the bus, we were besieged by little boys and
girls. At first I thought they were begging but then I heard them say,
"GI, you boom boom my sister? She number 1." When we brushed
them off, they said, "You number 10 GI." They continued to walk
along with us and became very annoying and persistant. Finally,
they gave up and turned away but not before calling us some vile
names. My first reaction was anger but I guess this was survival for
them. I couldn't imagine kids that age soliciting.

An Khe was about two blocks long and it was wall to wall
business. You could buy anything there from lunch to sex. It was a
center for the black market. U.S. military items were on every

stand. Uniforms and boots could be purchased on request and who knows what else. It was apparent that some U.S. military personnel were making a lot of money. Greenback dollars which were outlawed were everywhere and highly preferred.

Sin City-An Khe

Just adjacent to the town was Sin City. This was about fifty buildings built in a circle and all fenced in with barbed wire. There were MP's on the gate to check for passes and weapons. Inside the fencing, there were hundreds of prostitutes that had been imported from the larger cities to service the troops. Supposedly all of these girls were checked monthly for disease by the U.S. military.

The buildings were set up as bars with back rooms. The girls tried to dress and act western. There were small 45rpm record players blasting all the latest American songs. The girls knew just enough English to accomplish their negotiations or to cuss out a hard bargaining GI. The whole scenario was surreal. I didn't stay very long; this just wasn't my idea of sex. I knew that one trip to this place was enough for me and I really didn't like being without my weapon.

We spent the rest of the day going through the town looking at each stand and what they were selling. All the shopkeepers were fascinated with my self winding luminous wrist watch. They kept trying to buy or trade for it. Little did they know how important that watch was to me and my fellow troopers.

Kathleen had given me a small Zippo lighter for a going away present so I had it engraved with our names and 1966. The other guys made small purchases and seemed to enjoy bartering with the Vietnamese shopkeepers. The Vietnamese are an entrepreneurial people. They love to barter and trade and are generally good natured people.

We decided to have some lunch while we were in town so the guys selected a little restaurant. I wasn't as brave as they were about eating the local food so I just had a beer. We sat around and talked for awhile and then went back to base camp. I have to admit, I was glad to get back inside the perimeter of Camp Radcliff.

Our rest came to an end. We went back out to the field by CH-47 Chinook helicopters. This time we were headed for the An Loa Valley. The terrain was much different than Bong Son. It was more sparsely populated and more rain forest with lots of tree cover. It was thick jungle and we were following trails in column.

This was a very scary situation for the point men. The area was physically challenging as well. We were carrying extra ammo because of the terrain. I didn't like this place at all. I felt like we were going to run into a large force and wouldn't have artillery or air support. Visibility was minimal. If contact was made it would be close-in fighting.

We spent several days doing this and I think there was a time when we were lost. It might have been my imagination but I think for a while we were going in a circle. Fortunately nothing happened and we saw no indication of activity so we were pulled out and sent to Camp Hammond which was a forward base camp near Phu Cat. We were there for one day when A Company made significant contact and we were sent to reinforce them. By the time we made our air assault, it was over with. A Company had lost five troopers and had several wounded. They had destroyed an enemy camp and killed thirty VC. A Company was air lifted to an LZ for a rest and we stayed in the area with C Company and continued the mission.

After a three day rest, A Company rejoined us and the mission was expanded. There was sporadic contact but nothing major. On Thanksgiving Day, November 24th, A and C Companies made contact with a sizable force and we were air assaulted into a valley and a blocking position. Before we could establish our positions, artillery rounds started coming in on us. We were diving for cover anywhere we could.

Capt. Hitti was screaming over the radio to the artillery forward observer, "Cease fire! Cease fire!"

The fire mission ceased, but not before five 105mm artillery rounds had come in on us. Three troopers from the first platoon had been wounded by the shrapnel. Fortunately, the wounds were not life threatening and the casualties were quickly evacuated. It was amazing that nobody was killed.

We remained in a blocking position until elements of C Company linked up with us. A and C Companies had lost eight troopers and their combined wounded was twenty-seven. They had inflicted heavy casualties on the NVA 93rd Battalion. It was decided at this time that the battalion be airlifted to Camp Hammond and that elements of the 25th Division would take over the area and continue the mop up.

It was pouring down rain when we arrived at Hammond and there wasn't enough shelter for the battalion so we had to tough it out. It was Thanksgiving and the Army tries its best to give the troops the traditional dinner and this was no exception. At dinner time, I was guarding an injured NVA soldier. He was laying on the ground moaning. I really didn't know what was wrong with him. I covered him with a poncho and he looked at me and painfully nodded his appreciation. The intelligence people were supposed to come for him but I'd have to stay with him until they arrived.

Zep came over to me and said, "I'll spell you. Go get some chow."

I went through the serving line and got my dinner. I looked around for some shelter but there wasn't any. I squatted down next to a tent to eat my dinner. The rain was coming down harder now and I was racing to finish. The rain from my steel pot was washing the food off the paper plate faster than I could eat it. I did the best that I could and then returned to Zep and the prisoner.

Zep said, "He must have passed out cuz he's quiet now." I thanked Zep for taking my place so I could eat. He smiled and walked away.

A half hour later a jeep pulled up with an intelligence officer and his driver and said, "We're here to pick up the prisoner. Give my driver a hand getting him in the jeep." We picked him up and put him in the back of the jeep.

The driver said, "We won't get much out of him, sir. He's dead. They jumped in the jeep and took off. I stood there in the rain very bewildered. This was just how insignificant death was. I'll never forget that Thanksgiving, watching a man die.

The next day we were on the move again. B Company was air assaulted into the Kim Son Valley. Intelligence reports said that the 18th NVA Regiment was in the area. C Troop 1/9th was doing the recon and we were to make a sweep through the valley. The company was spread across the valley and moving on line. It had rained earlier and there was a fresh scent in the air from the fruit trees and everything seemed extra green. The cloud cover kept the heat down a bit and helped us move with our heavy gear.

About midday through our sweep, we could hear small arms fire to the north. Capt. Hitti was on the radio immediately and learned that a platoon from C Troop had come under heavy fire and was in need of help. Capt. Hitti dispatched the second platoon and the remaining platoons would link up as soon as possible. We now moved at a faster pace so that we wouldn't be too far behind the second platoon.

As the second platoon approached the hamlet of Phu Huu, they took AK47 fire from a concealed bunker inside one of the village huts. There was very little cover which hampered their mobility and both squads were pinned down. The machine gunner laid down a base of fire trying to neutralize the bunker. He was unsuccessful and was killed as he crawled forward to assist his squad leader. The fire fight went on for quite awhile before the bunker went silent.

Lt. Gibbons and Pfc. Lew Albanese

One of the squads moved forward toward the village and immediately came under heavy fire from their left flank. They had walked right into an inverted L shaped ambush and once again were pinned down. Pfc. Lew Albanese realized what had happened and noticed a drainage ditch on his left flank. The ditch was actually a fortified part of the ambush. Albanese entered the ditch and worked his way down the line killing six of its occupants. He ran out of ammunition and fixed his bayonet. He fought hand to hand combat and killed two more enemy soldiers before being killed himself. His heroic actions no doubt saved many lives.

Capt. Hitti and the rest of the company moved into Phu Huu. It was getting dark and there was a great degree of confusion. There were huey gunships overhead circling the village and firing their rockets and machine guns in support. There was a lot of tree cover in and around the village so the gunships did not have a good visual on us. All of a sudden, one of the gunships was firing its machine guns through the trees in our direction. Dirt and bark from the trees was flying everywhere as we ran for cover. Mike and I dove into one of the fortified huts. We stayed in the prone position until the firing ceased.

By now it was so dark that you couldn't see anything and we weren't sure where anyone was. There was sporadic gunfire to the north of the village. We heard artillery fire in that direction and assumed that the Captain had called for it as a perimeter defense.

We were inside the hut trying to figure out our next move. We determined the best thing we could do was hold our position until we heard from Zep or Sgt. Hartje. The small arms fire had ceased and it was now very quiet in the village.

Two hours went by and we still had not made contact with anyone. It was eerie not being able to see and not knowing where anyone was at or what was going on. There was always that great fear of being overrun or becoming separated from your unit and captured. To be captured was certain death by execution. The enemy took no low ranking prisoners south of the DMZ.

Another hour passed, and Mike said, "What do you think? Should we try to make contact?"

I said, "I think we better stay put. If the guys are as disconnected as we are, they're liable to be trigger happy."

He agreed and said, "I'm starving. How about you? I was thinking about trying to crawl over to our gear and grab some C's."

I told him that I didn't think that was a good idea but he said he had to eat something and he was gonna go for it. He grabbed my 45 pistol and crawled out into the dark. I couldn't believe he was going out there.

Mike was probably gone no more than twenty minutes but to me it seemed like hours. To be alone in that dark place, was frightening. The only thing to do in a situation like this is to think and naturally you think the worst. I heard a brushing sound and I clenched my M16.

I heard Mike whisper, "Bob, it's me. Do you hear me?" I responded and he crawled back into the hut.

He said, "I got two boxes of C's for us and I talked to Zep. Zep says stay put until morning and we'll regroup. Everything is okay."

He put a box of C's in my hands and we opened them blind not knowing what they were. It didn't matter, we would have eaten anything at that point. I thanked Mike for what he had done.

I told him, "You got some stones doin' that."

He laughed and said, "You know me when I'm hungry." Mike was a skinny as a rail but he sure liked to eat.

At the first light, we could see troops moving around the inside of the village. I grabbed my M16 and went out and found Sgt. Hartje and Zep. They said that we would be staying in the village for awhile and for Mike and I to hold our position and that there would be a log ship in shortly. They told me that we had KIA's and wounded to be medevaced. That was all the info they had and Zep said he'd keep us posted. The log shipped arrived and Mike went over and got us each a paper plate of hot food and a canteen cup full of hot black coffee. He said the medevac ships had come and removed the wounded and KIA's. He wasn't sure who they were or what platoons.

After we had been resupplied, Capt. Hitti called a company meeting and he told us of the casualties of the previous day. The six troopers who had been killed were from the first and second platoons. As he went through each of their names, his voice quivered with emotion. He spoke a little of each of the men and it was obvious that he truly cared. This is something that he would do everytime we lost someone. This time, I knew two of the troopers so I felt the same pain as everyone else. Steve Day and Lew Albanese had died. Steve had joined the company with Bill Gould, Rich Roderick and me. Lew, I had come to know through his outgoing and friendly personality. He was easy to like and always had something funny to say. I didn't know the other four troopers but Mike did and he was very depressed.

B Company had eleven troopers wounded in the battle. Sixty-seven of the NVA 18th regiment were killed and four wounded enemy soldiers had been captured. Several weapons were seized and one light machine gun. We all heard the details of what Lew Albanese had done and that he was going to be recommended for the Medal of Honor for his life saving heroism and courage. Many years later, I learned that Lew had been awarded the nation's highest decoration. A year and a half later Hector Colon became the second member of B Company to receive the Medal of Honor.

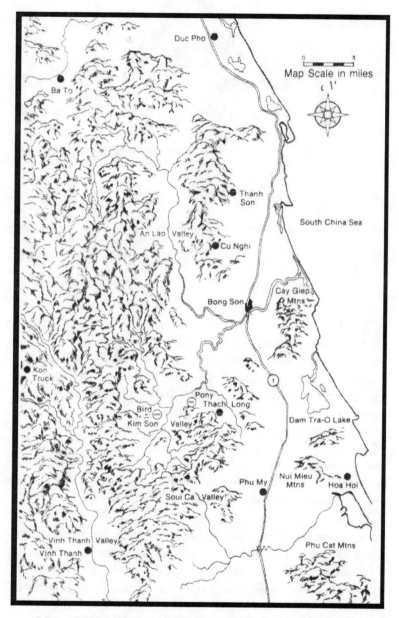

Map of Binh Dinh and Southern Quang Ngai Provinces

CHAPTER 8

The Green Line

We had very few pleasures in the bush. Smoking and drinking coffee were the big items. I had asked my mom if she could send me some decent instant coffee. She found these little foil packets of Hills Brothers instant coffee She would tape them flat inside a manila folder and then place the folder into a large manila envelope and mail it to me. I was from then on "the coffee man." Whenever we would get the time, I would take a quarter size ball of C4 plastic explosive and ignite it with a cigarette. I'd hold the canteen cup over it and within a minute we'd have hot coffee. We would pass the coffee around until it was gone. Everyone knew at mail call when I got more coffee.

I had terrific support from home. I got lots of mail, care packages, and anything that I could think of to make life a little better. I had a watch that glowed in the dark and a stainless steel mirror in a felt protector. These items were priceless and I shared them with all the guys around me. Some of the guys wrote my mother and thanked her personally for all the things she was sending. They were especially fond of the Fannie May candy that my family was sending. Small things in Vietnam were treasures to an infantry soldier.

I had been in Vietnam for over two months and I had learned a lot about how to survive. These are things you don't learn in training. Many things have to come out of experience. It has to become instinctive. Johnnie Gatlin, one of the replacements that came into the company with me, froze up in two different fire fights. He just stood there with bullets flying all around him. It's a wonder that he wasn't killed.

After those incidents, they pulled Gatlin out of the line platoon and sent him to the rear area for psychiatric evaluation. I never heard the results of that but I guess the Army wanted to make an example out of him. They kept him at the forward base camp burning shit with diesel fuel every day. This was probably one of the nastiest and sickening jobs the Army had. He told me that he didn't care and that he'd burn shit the rest of his tour but he'd get home. I don't know whether he was a coward or his fear in combat got the best of him. The mind is a fragile thing and I wouldn't pass judgment on him.

While we were at Camp Hammond, another incident occurred. We had just received more replacements. One of the replacements shot himself in the foot with a 45 automatic pistol. The wound was in between his ankle and his toes and was bad. Capt. Hitti and the man's platoon leader questioned him as to why he had done this. He told them that while he was back at Camp Radcliff, Sgt. Stanton had shown the replacements some of the bloody steel helmets with bullet holes. He told them that this is what they could expect when they went out in the field. The soldier said that he was afraid and figured that he'd wound himself bad enough to get out of Vietnam. We heard that there would be a second court martial charge against Stanton. I don't know what happened to the young soldier but he had messed up his foot pretty badly.

For the next week, we continued our search and destroy mission around the Phu Cat Massifs. It seemed as if the enemy had just disappeared into the tree covered highlands. They had been heavily decimated in Operation Irving, Thayer I, and the first part of Thayer II. Other than an occasional sniper, things were uneventful and that was a good thing.

Mike Speck, Bob Powers, and Pete Ross

John "Zep" Zepeda and Jim McLarren

We were exhausted from combat, slogging through the rice paddies, the heat, and the monsoon season. The brigade command decided to give us a welcomed rest. On the 8th of December, the battalion was placed on perimeter guard of the division base camp at An Khe. This was going to be nice duty, thirty days of guard in a relatively safe place. We would be here at Christmas and that was fantastic.

The perimeter of Camp Radcliff was known as the Green Line. The Green Line was huge and took the better part of the battalion to man it. There were guard towers every fifty yards. The field of vision to the front had been cleared of foliage and had several rings of concertina barbed wire. There were booby traps and claymore mines.

Pete Ross, Jim McLarren, and I were assigned to one of two towers that were located on a small sandbar island. Randy, Mike, and Rich were assigned to the other. The only access to the island was a rickety rope foot bridge that swayed violently as you crossed it. These two towers were probably the most remote on the line but this had an upside. We probably wouldn't have much company.

At least once a day, a huey would fly past the towers at almost eye level. The officer of the guard would make certain that the tower was manned and everything was in order.

I was on guard early one morning when I saw a command jeep pull up to the rope bridge. An officer jumped out and started to cross the rickety bridge. He got about ten feet out and decided to go back. He got in his jeep and drove off. An hour passed and a huey appeared on the horizon. The chopper flew in by our tower and set down within fifty feet. A major hopped off and came over to the tower and climbed up the ladder. I recognized him as our battalion XO, Major Jennings.

I saluted him with, "Garry Owen, sir."

He smiled at me and said, "Private, you didn't think that bridge would stop me. Did you?"

"No sir," I responded.

He proceeded to inspect our machine gun, searchlight, and ask a series of questions regarding our defense mechanisms.

I answered his questions and he said, "Good job, Powers. Everything is in order. Garry Owen, trooper," as he saluted me.

He climbed down from the tower and made his way over to the other island tower.

Each guard tower had three men and had to be manned twenty-four seven. There was a radio, an M60 machine gun, and a big searchlight. The towers were about fifteen feet high and had a good field of vision. The platform was about six feet square and the tower had a corrugated tin roof for sun and rain protection. They were also sandbagged for more protection from small arms fire.

Out to the front of each position, there was triple concertina barbed wire, claymore mines, and different types of booby traps. During the daylight hours, we had to make daily perimeter inspections to see if anything had been disturbed. One man per tower could leave the tower during the day for whatever reason so it was like having every third day off.

The Army paid Vietnamese civilians to keep the front of the perimeter clear of vegetation. Whenever this would occur, two of us would have to go out and keep an eye on them and make sure that they did not get into any of the ordinance or plant any traps for us.

One day Randy and I were out there watching about twenty civilians clearing vegetation with machetes. All of a sudden a woman let out a loud scream and begins to wail and cry. A man, apparently her husband, walked calmly over to a rock and sat down. Less than a minute later, he fell over dead. I signaled for the interpreter to come over to me.

I said to him, "What's going on?"

He said to me, "Snake bite him. He know he die so he sit down. I kill snake."

His wife cried over his body and two men put him on an ox cart and they pulled him away. The other people kept working as if nothing had happened. Randy and I just stood there in disbelief. Death in Vietnam was just that simple.

I got a chance to catch up on my mail and write some overdue letters. At mail call, I got a fruit cake from my Aunt Jean and a two pound box of Fannie May candy from my uncle John. The boys were overjoyed, especially Mike and Pete Ross. They said they never had chocolate as good as that. Mike sat down and wrote my mom a letter of thanks.

Mike Speck's thank you letter to my mother

I opened a letter from Kathleen and read through it savoring every line. She could even be provocative and sexy in a letter. I closed my eyes and I pictured her in my mind. I could smell the lavender in her hair and her perfume. I could see her mischievous smile and I could taste her kiss. What I wouldn't give to be out of this hellhole and with her.

Sgt. Hartje came to our island tower positions to see how we were doing. He gave the towers and our defenses a thorough check and made us aware of how important perimeter defense was. The VC were making more and more night probes. He liked the way we had things setup. The sergeant was a thin wiry built man. Most of the guys called him "Pops." He was a real heartland type and had a fatherly manner about him. This was his third war as an infantry soldier. To say the least, he was the real deal.

I brewed up some coffee for us and the Sergeant started to fill us in on the latest news. He told us that, our battalion commander, LTC. Swett, had become ill and was forced to return to the states for treatment. We were sad to hear that because the Colonel was well respected by everyone in the battalion. He had brought these guys through training and to Vietnam. I didn't know him but what I heard from the guys was good enough for me. Our new CO was LTC. Canham. There was going to be an installation ceremony in our battalion area. Two of us would have to attend in full battle uniform the following day. Randy being in charge of our tower would remain behind and Mike and I would attend the ceremony.

The next day, Mike and I reported to the battalion parade field for the installation ceremony. Gen. William Westmoreland personally installed LTC. Canham. He gave a lengthy speech on how he had served under the Colonel's father, Major General Canham in the 82nd Airborne Division during WWII. He went on to praise our new Colonel and to let us know how lucky we were to have him and what a great leader he was. It is interesting how this played out over the next two months.

The ceremony being complete, we headed back to our tower. We filled Randy in and resumed our daily routine. The weather was hot and clear but it was nice when there was no search and destroy missions to deal with. We made several improvements to our position for both defense and comfort. We had a two man tent and two air mattresses which seemed luxurious compared to our normal life style. Sanitation was still crude but the water around the island gave us a place to bathe and wash our clothes. After three months in Vietnam, I had gotten used to the squalid conditions but that's not to say that I liked them. When looking around the base camp at different jobs, it was apparent that we had the worst.

I have always maintained that the physical and hygienic hardships were almost as bad as the combat. A case in point was my friend, Jim Pitzen. Jim was passing blood in his stool and he told me about it. I asked him if he had spoken to any of our leaders about it. He said no. I told him to go talk to the Lieutenant about it. He came back later and said the Lieutenant made light of it and said that the condition would probably pass.

I decided to go to the Lieutenant and talk to him about it. I approached the Lieutenant and asked him for a minute. I ran through Jim's story and right away I could tell there was an attitude problem. It was like, why don't you mind your own business.

He said to me, "And your medical expertise is?"

I admitted that it was zero but passing blood was serious and it could become a bigger problem out in the bush. I think I got him thinking but I was on his shit list.

Jim was coming up on his R&R and I suggested that he go on sick call to 15th Medical when he came back. I told him he needed to find out what the problem was before coming back out in the bush. It seemed that the higher ups would rather ignore these problems than lose a man. We were under strength but that's a different problem and required a different solution.

Christmas week was at hand and there would be shows that we could see. On the 21st of December, the 70th Engineer Battalion had a USO show at their Frontier Club. They had a Japanese singer named Patty Yuri who was accompanied by a violin and an accordion. She was an excellent singer. She sang many of our favorites: " Exodus, Together Again, I Left My Heart in San Francisco, Chicago," and many others. It was a great time and a reminder of home.

On Christmas Eve, Billy Graham had a special service for us and afterward a great talk. This was the first time that I had heard Billy Graham speak and I was impressed. He is truly a man of God.

On the 26th of December 1966, I got to see the Bob Hope Show. I remember it like it was yesterday. I can see Bob walking around on the stage with his golf club cracking joke after joke. He poked fun at our commanding general, MG. John Norton. I remember the cast as: Joey Heatherton, Anita Bryant, Vic Damone,

Phyllis Diller, Jerry Colona, the Korean Kittens, and Miss World – Rita Faria from Bombay, India. I had a great view from in front of a jeep standing up on the bumper. To watch all these great performances and to see all these beautiful women was great. I had never seen a show like this.

On the 29th of December, our battalion was pulled off Green Line duty one week early. An artillery position known as LZ Bird in the Kim Son Valley was attacked by three battalions of the 22nd NVA Regiment at 1:00 am. LZ Bird was an artillery firebase with two batteries and defended by an under strength company from the 1st of the 12th Cavalry. The north end of the LZ was breached and a horrific battle ensued. Some of the gun positions were overrun. The 16th Field Artillery leveled their howitzers and fired beehive rounds into the human wave assaults. They reloaded and fired again shredding the enemy with 8500 projectiles per round. The battle lasted for two hell filled hours and the enemy fled in defeat.

The sunrise of the following day showed the carnage of battle. Of the 199 defenders, 27 had been killed and 67 wounded. There were 266 NVA bodies and blood ran in the trenches. C & D companies of the 1st Bn. of the 8th Cavalry were air assaulted in to relieve the battered company and to pursue the fleeing NVA. Almost constant contact was maintained and another 211 enemy were killed in the retaliatory pursuit. Another bit of irony, B Company 5/7 had secured LZ Bird several times and I left there on December 8th to go on Green Line duty. Sometimes luck is in the cards.

Our battalion was air assaulted into LZ Jacky on the 29th of December and B Company was to secure the LZ and A & C Companies would go into a blocking position in case the 22nd NVA Regiment tried to flee to the south. We would rotate our position with a sister company in a few days. The next few days of perimeter defense were very scary. The nights seemed long and our eyes wearied from staring out into the blackness expecting a night attack. When we heard about the human wave attack at LZ Bird, we all wondered if it was our turn.

Four days went by and we rotated with C Company. We were back in the bush again. I had become spoiled at Camp Radcliff. We were in the Soui Ca Valley also known to us as Happy Valley. It was anything but happy. The terrain was miserable and was only matched by the weather. The valley was very dense and had very little population. It was slow going and required a lot of machete work in order to stay off the main trails. Leaches were a big problem in this area. I was fortunate that I could feel them when they got on me. A couple drops of our mosquito repellant and they dropped right off. I saw insects that I had never seen before and hope never to see again. The city boy didn't like all this outdoor living. A nice desk job would've suited me.

The good news was that this valley seemed to be pacified. There were no signs of VC or NVA. We had some engineers with us and they blew up any old bunkers or anything else the enemy might use. The NVA had paid dearly at LZ Bird. They had lost a lot of personnel and equipment and had retreated to the tree covered highlands to resupply and that would take time. One thing is for sure, Charlie would come back and fight another day.

Randy Ganhinhin, Fred Scheimreif, Julio Torres,
Jim Haggerty, and Pete Ross

CHAPTER 9

R&R in Hawaii

At the time, it was a given that only officers went to Hawaii on R&R. This was so they could meet their wives there. The other choices were Tokyo, Taipei, Singapore, Kuala Lumpur, Bangkok, Manila or Hong Kong. It was expected that enlisted men would make a choice from this group. Several guys had gone on R&R and through them I had the picture of what each of these places had to offer. I really wasn't interested in any of them and Asia surely wasn't high on my list. Randy had gone to Hawaii on his R&R because he was from Honolulu. This was the only exception that had been made. I decided that I was going to Hawaii and that I wouldn't take no for an answer. My reasoning was that everyone there spoke English and it was as far away from Vietnam as I could get. Crossing the international dateline gave me an extra day so that was reason enough.

Mike and I were in our foxhole position when Zep came down with a clipboard and asked Mike where he wanted his R&R. Mike's first choice was Taipei and then Bangkok or Tokyo. Zep noted it and then asked me. I said Hawaii, Hawaii, and Hawaii.

He looked at me and said, "You know that's not gonna fly."

I told him to just put it down. He wrote it down and walked away shaking his head.

Mike laughingly said, "Now you went and did it. That'll start some shit."

I said I didn't care and I didn't see any reason that I couldn't go to Hawaii.

January was turning out to be a quiet month. The Viet Cong and the NVA were avoiding contact with the Cavalry and were probably in dire need of rebuilding. They had taken heavy casualties and lost lots of weapons, food, and medical supplies. The wounded NVA soldiers had to be a logistical nightmare for the enemy.

The major offensive attack at LZ Bird had taken place directly after the Christmas truce and was a pattern that I would witness many times in my tour. None of us understood why there would be any truce when it was a known fact that it was NVA resupply time. We knew that the period following any truce would be followed by more aggressive offensive attacks. The Ho Chi Minh Trail was a hub of activity during these periods. The enemy was being provided a window of opportunity and it was being used to full advantage. Geographically, the Ho Chi Minh Trail running through two supposedly neutral countries and stretching the length of Vietnam was perfect for resupply. At that time, the U.S. was not crossing into Cambodia or Laos with ground troops.

The battalion was operating along Highway One near Phu Cat and B Company was occupying a small abandoned hamlet. It had been occupied before and all the fortifications were in place. Three platoons would sweep the area around Phu Cat and my platoon would secure the hamlet and company CP.

Mike had left on his R&R to Taipei so Rich and I were teamed up in a bunker. During the day we improved our position and by night we rotated guard. We had time to catch up on our letter writing and Rich got a little card playing time in. He was a good poker player and he loved to brag about it but I had to give him that. He told me that he was also the best at pool. I believed him after watching him win at cards.

Rich and I were in our position cleaning our M16s when our platoon leader, the Lieutenant, came over. I knew something was up because it was out of the norm for him to be looking in on us.

He said to me, "Powers, I understand there's a problem with your R&R choice."

I replied, "No sir, not that I'm aware of. I gave my three choices to Zep."

His demeanor changed and he snapped, "I'm gonna ask you again what your choices are and I expect them all to be different."

I gave him my three choices, "Hawaii, Hawaii, and Hawaii."

By now his face was red and he said, "You're a real smart ass."

I told him that I wasn't being disrespectful, just giving him my choices.

He came back at me with, "You keep that up and you won't get any R&R and it will be your own damn fault."

We stood there looking at each other for a moment. He realized that I wasn't going to say anymore and he stormed off. That was strike two for me with him.

Rich looked up at me and shook his head.

He laughed and said, "I don't think that was the smartest thing you've ever done. He's gonna have it in for you and what if you don't get R&R?"

I said, "We'll see about that. All I know is, those are my choices and I don't see why I'm any different than him. He puts his pants on the same as me. If I don't get R&R, then so be it."

Rich laughed again and said, "You are one hard headed Irishman. I hope he don't have it in for you."

Later that day Sgt. Hartje came over and talked to me about R&R. I explained to him that I wasn't trying to piss anybody off. I just wanted to go to Hawaii and if I couldn't go there, I didn't want anything. I think he read my sincerity.

"I'll talk to the Lieutenant. It'll all work out."

A few days passed and Mike came back from Taipei. He said he had a great time and he really liked Taiwan. He had booked a girl for his stay and she was his constant companion. The only problem he ran into was the language barrier. The Chinese girl that he was with didn't speak much English. He bought this little pocket translation book and between that and sign language was how they communicated. He was hell bent on writing her and it was no easy chore. He said he'd like to go back and see her after his tour. The poor guy had fallen for this girl. I wanted to say something but I just couldn't hurt his feelings.

Mike hadn't had the easiest home life. He came from a broken home and he was searching for something. From the little that he told me, none of it sounded good. I noticed that when we lost someone in battle, he took it exceptionally hard. It was almost like he had lost family. Maybe this was his family. I was afraid to go there with him. At this point, I realized how much family influenced our behavior and inner strength.

The Lieutenant left for his R&R and the tension was relieved temporarily. I hadn't heard any more about mine and I knew better than to ask. I had resigned myself to the fact that I might not get one but I had a secret weapon. I didn't care.

Another week of drudgery passed in the field. Sgt. Hartje strolled up to me with a grin on his weathered face.

"Powers, pack your gear. You're on the next log ship to An Khe. You're going on R&R to Hawaii. Well,… what the hell are ya waitin' for?"

I thanked him and gathered up my gear. He never said so but I knew he had a hand in it. Everyone respected him and his opinion, especially the Lieutenant.

I got back into An Khe late that afternoon. I got cleaned up and had a hot meal in the new mess hall that the battalion had named after 1st Sgt. Hare. They had a plaque made up with his name and dates on it and it was placed in front of the door.

I ran into Rod, the company clerk, and he gave me the low down on R&R.

He said, "I almost feel like I know you after all that commotion over Hawaii. Good for you, you got what you wanted. I agree with you that everyone should have full choice. Stop by the CQ after you eat and I'll have your orders ready."

I went over to the CQ and Rod had my paperwork ready. He explained everything to me. The next morning I would be flying to Cam Ranh Bay and the R&R staff would take it from there. I went back into the storage area and dug my duffel bag out. I grabbed my shaving gear and some civilian clothing. I would be gone for six heavenly days and I was happy that I had everything that I needed. I wouldn't have to waste time shopping in Hawaii. It would all be fun time. I was really looking forward to seeing Hawaii and excited knowing that I could talk to everyone without hand signals.

The bus for the Golf Course (Camp Radcliff's air strip) would be at the battalion area at 7am. I had a little time to go over to the 70th Engineer's EM club and have a few cold beers. They had their club fixed up nice with memorabilia from home. It's surprising how that type of thing takes your mind off the everyday and into a field of good memories. I started to think of home. Eight more months of hell and I'd be out of here and back to the place that I loved. I got some tokens from the bartender and went to the juke box. They had all the latest songs and I started dropping the tokens in. I picked out some my favorites:"When a Man Loves a Woman, Barefootin', Poor Side of Town, Sunshine Superman, and See You in September."

I thought the last song summed up my story. If only it was September. All of these songs reminded me of Kathleen and all the fun we had while I was home on leave. I wished that I could see her in Hawaii but that was impossible.

I finished my beer and walked out into the humid night. I could see the orange flashes and hear the rumbling of the H&I artillery fire in the distance. No matter where you were in Vietnam, you were never too far from the war. I walked along the dark dirt road back to the battalion area thinking about tomorrow. I was always thinking about tomorrow, that's what kept me going.

The few beers made me sleep sound. I woke up at the first light and went outside to the make shift shower. What a great feeling to have water streaming all over my body and be able to use soap. I washed my hair and shaved. I even got to put on some after shave cologne and combed my hair. I got dressed in my Class A uniform and I almost felt normal. It was a strange feeling to have that uniform and shoes on in the middle of a Vietnam war zone.

I went over to the battalion mess hall and the cook asked me what I wanted to eat. I chose fried eggs, bacon, toast, orange juice, and coffee. It was really nice to be able to sit down at a table and eat. I had such a good feeling inside. This day was off to a real good start and the thought of leaving here made it even better.

The bus rolled up at 7am and I was on my way. There were quite a few guys on the bus and we were making stops along the way picking up more. I looked out the window at Hong Con Mountain and all the different battalion areas that we were passing along the way. When we got to the air strip, there was a C130 waiting for us. Within a half hour, we were airborne and on our way to Cam Ranh Bay. It was a short flight and we arrived at the R&R center in less than an hour. Those of us that were heading for Hawaii were called from a roster and grouped for a commercial flight that would be leaving within the hour. I would say that almost everyone in the group was an officer. I did feel a little uncomfortable, but then I thought, who cares what they think.

We boarded a United Airline jet and I was seated all the way at the back of the plane. I didn't care just as long as I was on the plane. I had a window seat and I liked that. Before long it was time for take off. Two pretty little stewardesses sat down next to me.

"Sir, we will be seated next to you for take off and landings if you don't mind." Both of them had big smiles and I knew they could read my mind. I hadn't been this close to girls this pretty in four months. We introduced ourselves and I found out their names were Marge and Dolly. They were both asking me questions about myself and it really made me feel good. I definitely had the best seat on the plane. No war stories, just guy girl talk and I was loving it. We reached our altitude and the smoking light came on. The girls had work to do so they went back to the galley and brought out the refreshment cart. Marge, the stewardess that was seated next to me, asked me what I would like to drink. She fixed me a VO and water and flipped me a couple bags of cashews. I also got a sweet smile.

After the refreshment round was completed, Marge came back and sat down again.

She said, "Are you meeting your wife in Hawaii?"

I told her that I was single and all my reasons for wanting to go to Hawaii instead of the Orient. She laughed and said she didn't blame me. She asked me if I was an officer. She was surprised when I told her that I was a private.

She replied "Most of the guys on these Hawaii runs are officers on their way to meet the wives. What are you going to do in Hawaii?"

I told her sleep, good food, Canadian whiskey, and air conditioning were some of my high priorities. Whatever else that comes my way is a bonus. Marge went on to tell me that she was from Bethany, Oklahoma and that she had taken her stewardess training in Elk Grove, Illinois. I told her that I was an electrician and that I had worked on the security system at that school. Dolly came over and told Marge that it was time do lunch. Marge excused herself and they went into the galley.

Shortly the food cart came out with Dolly and another girl heading up front toward 1st class. Marge came out of the galley with a single tray for me.

She winked and smiled and said, "Special service for a special guy."

She had also made me another VO and water. I thanked her as she turned and went back in the galley. This was a nice lunch. There was fried chicken, mashed potatoes, gravy, and green beans. It even smelled good and, of course, I was hungry. I was by myself as I ate so I was done very quickly. I pulled a magazine from the seat pouch and began flipping through it. There was lots of Hawaii info and I had to start putting together some kind of a plan. I needed to find a place to stay with the amenities that I was looking for. I jotted down some motels and restaurants that appealed to me. I would have to call home for money. I knew that what I had wouldn't get me through six days.

After lunch was over, the Captain came over the speakers and announced that we would be landing at Anderson AFB in Guam to let off some passengers and to take on some additional fuel. We would be staying on the aircraft as it would only be a half hour delay. The seat belt and no smoking lights came on as we began our descent. Marge and Dolly returned to their seats next to me and we resumed our conversation. The girls were very interested in Chicago nightlife so I did my best to point out some of the hot spots on Rush Street, downtown, and Old Town. I told them that I didn't spend a lot of time in these places but occasionally my friends and I would go there. They said that they needed to expand their horizons in Chicago. Chicago was United's hub and they would be spending most of their free time there.

We touched down at Anderson AFB and turned to taxi back to the terminal. I gazed out my window and I saw row after row of B52 bombers. Each was protected by a U-shaped masonry enclave. This was the main B52 support wing for Vietnam. It was a very impressive sight. It would be hard to imagine the hellfire that all these bombers were capable of. The girls released their seat belts and went about their duties and I kicked back for a little nap.

It seemed like just minutes and I felt the plane begin to move. The girls came back and strapped in for takeoff.

Marge looked at me and said, "Last leg of the flight, I'll bet your anxious to get to Honolulu." I told her that I was and that I was looking forward to some fun and rest. I was feeling a little apprehensive about where I would stay and what I would do while I was there. I thought about grabbing a flight to O'Hare and spending my time at home. That seemed like a good idea. I'd make a phone call when we got to Hawaii. I closed my eyes and drifted off to happy thoughts of Chicago and, of course, Kathleen.

A couple hours passed and I awoke to the rattling of the dinner cart. Marge poked her head around the corner of the partition and asked me what my dinner preference was. She suggested the beef sirloin and I nodded my approval. I was really hungry and the dinner wasn't bad for airline food. Marge came by after dinner and sat down and told me we'd be in Hawaii in an hour and a half. I thanked her for keeping me company on the flight. She said that I looked liked I needed a little company. I really did feel a little out of place being the only enlisted man on the flight. Getting this seat on the plane helped put me at ease or at least made me feel a little less obvious.

The Captain came over the radio and announced that we'd be arriving at Honolulu International Airport in fifteen minutes and gave the time and temperature. It had been a long flight and I would be glad to have my feet on terra firma again. We landed and I said my thanks and goodbyes to Marge and Dolly.

Marge gave me a wink and said, "Good luck, soldier."

I left the aircraft and went into the terminal to scout out a telephone. I called home and my brother answered. I told him where I was and that I had thoughts of flying home. He said that I could put that idea to rest as they were in the middle of a twenty-three inch blizzard. Chicago had come to a full stop. He said that he and my mother were lucky to make it home from downtown.

My family passed the phone around and each member gave me the latest news. It was really great talking to them after four months. When I spoke to my mother, I could feel her joy knowing that I would be out of harms way for the next week. I promised to call often while I was in Hawaii.

I left the airport and took a bus to Waikiki Beach. What a beautiful sight the beach was with Diamondhead in the background. The Pacific was the most beautiful dark blue and almost turquoise near the white sand beach. The sweet smell of the ocean completed the picture.

I had to find a place to stay and I had a couple of options. I could stay at Ft. DeRussy for free or seek a hotel or motel. I elected to go for the latter as I didn't want to be reminded of the Army. I found a nice motel on Kuhio Avenue which was about one block from the beach. I paid the bill in advance and went to my room. I hit the shower and slept for a couple of hours.

It was dark outside when I woke up. I checked the time and got dressed. It was a balmy night and I decided to walk down to the beach. I walked along Kalakaua Avenue taking in all the sights.

I got to the beach and took my shoes and socks off and walked along the shoreline. The surf washed in and it felt great on my feet. It was so peaceful and serene, a far cry from Army life and Nam. Just to be away from that filth and misery was indescribable. I wondered to myself how I ever got into this mess. I sat down on the sand and faced the ocean. I listened to sounds of the ocean. This was a great place to do a little thinking about the future. I had no idea what to do with my time here but I was determined to make the best of it.

I got up and started to walk again. I noticed lights up ahead and I could hear Polynesian music. As I got closer, I could see a bar and a stage with live entertainment. I put my shoes back on and walked up to the bar and ordered a beer. I spun around on my stool and faced the stage. There was a Samoan fire dance taking place and it was good. The dancers were in South Pacific costumes and the music was very lively. The name of this place was the Queen Surf, it was a mecca of entertainment. There were four bars and two restaurants. This was a place to check out more thoroughly later on. I finished my beer and continued my beach tour. I was off to a good start but I was tired and decided to pack it in for the night.

I got up with the birds the next morning and had a nice breakfast. I went to see the Punchbowl Crater and then back to the beach for a little sun and surf. I found myself a nice spot on the beach and sat down. I watched more pretty girls in bikinis than I could count. I needed some female companionship but I wasn't comfortable in the world of surfing and beautiful suntans. Somehow this just wasn't me. I was disappointed about not being able to go home but I supposed that it was for the best. I probably wouldn't have wanted to go back to Vietnam after a taste of home.

By the end of day three, I was beginning to get bored with Hawaii. This is a great place for a honeymoon or a vacation for a married couple. Lonely was the word of the day. My phone calls home were the highlight of the day. Sightseeing, eating, and the like are a whole lot better when they're shared with someone.

I was beginning to think my choice wasn't the best but on the other hand what did the others have to offer? Sex was probably the only difference. Prostitutes didn't interest me and I was afraid of all the unknown STD's. I'd just have to stick to my original agenda and enjoy the luxury and safety of Waikiki Beach.

At the end of day four, I decided to go to the Queen Surf and have a big steak dinner and then try their piano bar for a few drinks. I bought myself a new shirt and pants that afternoon and thought it might put me more in the Polynesian spirit. I showered and shaved and headed to the Queen Surf. I went into the restaurant and was seated with an ocean view. I ordered my steak and a glass of red wine. The dinner was all that I had hoped for and I took my sweet time eating. I went into the piano bar and took a seat at the bar. I figured I'd have a couple VO and waters and finish out the night.

I had just got my first drink when I heard someone say, "Hey soldier, haven't we met before?" I turned and there was Marge standing there with a big smile on her face. She looked gorgeous. Her black hair was down to her shoulders and she had an orange dress on that was just right for her. She looked so different from her stewardess uniform. I realized that she was a lot taller than I thought.

She told me she was with Dolly and her husband at a table. She asked me if I cared to join them. I picked my drink up and followed her to the table. Dolly greeted me and introduced me to her husband, Tate, who was a United pilot. I was so happy to have someone to talk to. They told me they were on their turnaround break and that they'd be going back to the mainland in a few days. I said I'd be glad to trade with them as I'd be heading west in two days. We were all talking a mile a minute but I kept looking at Marge. Her eyes were almost black and almond shaped. She had an exotic look.

Marge wanted to take advantage of the music and dance. I warned her about my dancing skills and she just laughed. It was a slow song and she got very close to me and I inhaled the scent of her perfume. Marge had it all together and she knew it. She was femininity personified. Two hours with her and all the loneliness that I'd experienced the past three days was gone. We went back to the table and Tate and Dolly said that they had to go and asked me if I would see Marge back to her hotel. I said that I'd be glad to. I was just happy that the night wasn't over. I found Marge so easy to talk to. She asked me a lot about my life and seemed to be interested in every word. She told me that she was English, Spanish, and Cherokee. That accounted for her good looks. She said that she had wanted to be a stewardess since the first time she flew.

I replied, "I think you made a good choice because you're very good at it."

We finished our drinks and she said, "I think we better go."

I paid the tab and we walked out into the balmy Waikiki night. As we walked up the avenue, I felt like I had a life again. Vietnam was far away in my mind.

She said, "I'm staying at the Waikiki Hilton. United keeps rooms there for us when we're held over."

She asked me where I was staying and I told her. She reached down and held my hand and it felt so natural. It was like I had known her for a long time.

We got to the hotel entrance and she looked at me and said, "Would you like to come up and have a nightcap?"

"Only if you twist my arm," I laughingly replied. She gave me a big smile and a two handed arm twist.

I never left her room that night.

The next morning, I woke up and Marge was lying next to me with her head by my neck. I thought about the night before and all that happened and what a good time that we had. Her eyes opened and she looked at me.

"Good morning, Bob."

"Hey"

"Did you sleep good?"

I smiled at her and said, "Never better."

What do you feel like doing today?"

" I would like to spend the day doing all the things that you like to do."

"I would like to stay right here and order breakfast in."

"And then what?"

"You know!"

In the evening we went back to the Queen Surf and did a little dancing and a lot of talking. We walked the beach and sat on the breakwater. This was my last night in Hawaii and I think that Marge was trying to make it my best. We made it back up to her room and I fixed us some drinks and we sat out on the balcony facing the ocean. What a sight from that balcony. Ten stories up and a full moon, we could see Diamondhead on the left, the lights of Waikiki, every type of marine vessel from a catamaran to ocean going yachts. This was life at its very best. We talked for a long time and then she stood and pulled me inside.

"C'mon." She had that special look in her eye.

The next morning when I awoke, there was a beautiful breeze flowing in through the balcony door. Marge was up and at the door. She had ordered breakfast from room service. I got up and threw a robe on and joined her. She was even stunning with no make up. I looked at her and wished it would never end but today was the day. I now know why guys go AWOL. I told her today was my return day and that I had to be at the airport by 2:00. I was pretty quiet through breakfast and she asked me if something was wrong. I had never told her what my job was in Nam and I didn't want to now. I just told her how much fun that I'd had with her and that I didn't want it to end. I thanked her for turning things around for me. If it wasn't for her, Hawaii would have been a disaster.

Marge got a United courtesy car and took me over to the motel and I got my things. We drove to Honolulu Airport and I told her I wanted her to write me and maybe after my tour......

She interrupted me and said, "Bob, I can't. I haven't been honest with you. I have a husband back in Oklahoma. I wanted to tell you but I couldn't. I wanted what we had even if it wasn't meant to be."

I was speechless. I felt pain where I never felt pain before. When we got to the airport, I had a hard time getting goodbye out.

She scooted over and gave me a kiss and said, "I'm sorry if I hurt you. That was never my intention." She wished me good luck and I said goodbye and walked into the airport.

CHAPTER 10

Back in Country

I guess that's one part of life that I will never understand. One minute you're on top and the next you're looking up from the abyss. I went through the motions at the airport and boarded my flight without thinking about where I was going. I hoped that I could sleep most of the way or maybe the damn plane would break down or something great like that. I think leaving Hawaii was almost as hard as leaving home. The difference was that I knew what was waiting for me this time.

I closed my eyes and tried to sleep but I kept thinking about Marge and my last two days in Hawaii. I was feeling sorry for myself and I knew I had to turn it around. I should be thinking about all the positive things and what she had done for me. She had made a good memory for me and one that I would remember all my life. She had read me like an open book and her timing couldn't have been better. I just couldn't get the "why" out of my head.

The flight back was uneventful and way too fast. I did manage to get some sleep. I spent the rest of the time thinking and trying to sort everything out. I remember that hollow empty feeling that I had on that return flight. A person would have to be a nut case to want to return to combat. Tasting the good life and the touch of a beautiful woman didn't make it any easier. I guess knowing the pain was better than the alternative.

The plane touched down in Cam Ranh Bay and taxied up to the terminal. I stepped out onto the steps into the blazing sun and the humidity that was Vietnam. The heat was like getting hit with a hammer. After knowing this climate, I knew that I'd always be a snowbird. At that moment, I wished that I was back in the "Chi-town" with a snow shovel in hand.

We had a half hour wait until we boarded a C130 for Camp Radcliffe. A short hop to Radcliffe and a bus ride and I was back in the battalion area. The bus rolled to a stop in front of B Company and I hopped off. I walked into the orderly room and Rod and Capt. Hitti were sitting there talking. Capt. Hitti looked up at me.

"Well, Powers, how was Hawaii?" He had a grin on his face as if he knew something. He and Rod were close so I'm sure he knew all about the Hawaii fiasco. I told them that I had a good time and got lots of rest.

The Captain told me that Sgt. Hartje had to go back to the States on emergency leave and that I had a new platoon sergeant, Sgt. Thompson. He said he that seems like a good guy and that we all needed to show him the ropes because he hadn't seen any combat. He also told me that the Lieutenant had been reassigned as an aide to the Colonel.

"See what happens when you're gone for a week? Everything goes to hell," he laughed.

I changed into my jungle fatigues, stowed my Class A and civies, and gathered all my field gear. I sat down on an empty cot with a stack of mail that Rod had given me. Maybe I could read them all and answer a few before the log ship arrived. I was working my way through the stack anticipating a letter from Kathleen. I was disappointed when I got to the last letter and it wasn't from her.

Rod poked his head into the tent and yelled, "Hey Bob, Capt. Hitti wants to see you."

I walked up to the orderly room and went in. Capt. Hitti was seated at his desk and he waived me to an empty chair.

He looked at me and said, "You won't be going out to the field on the log ship this afternoon. 1st Sgt. Sipple and Rod have need of your able bodied assistance. You probably could use a little decompression time anyhow."

That was good news. My assignment was to straighten up all the platoon tents and to clean two of our three 81mm. mortars. The platoon would only be carrying one tube but a lot more ammo on our next mission. I would be able to answer those letters and have a couple peaceful days before returning to the company. Even a couple days of cleanup was heaven compared to the misery of the field. The odd jobs stretched into three days. I didn't mind at all; the meter was running.

I rejoined the company on February 4th at LZ Ruby. I introduced myself to the new platoon sergeant. We talked for a few moments.

Zep walked up and said, "Hey Bob, how's the Hawaii kid? He's one of mine, Sarge. I'll square him away."

I followed Zep to the other side of the LZ and I saw Mike sitting with his legs dangling into a foxhole and writing a letter.

Zep said, "Hey Mike, look what I found. Geez' I hope your ma sent some coffee. We ain't had a decent cup of coffee since you left."

I reached into my leg pocket and flipped a plastic bag of coffee packets to Zep.

"Now we're talkin. Mike, ball the C4 and we'll have a cup."

Before the coffee was done, Rich and Doc came by. We passed the cup around and I got quizzed about Hawaii. I didn't say much, just the usual. I didn't want to talk about Marge.

The guys filled me in on the happenings while I was gone. I asked them about our new platoon sergeant and they all just rolled their eyes. They said he wasn't a bad guy but super green. Apparently, he had been shipped from the states with no Vietnam training. To his credit, he wasn't gung ho and he was willing to listen to his more experienced squad leaders. Vietnam was a dangerous place for a newcomer that didn't want to listen. The fact that we didn't have a lieutenant didn't help him either.

Things had been pretty decent for the battalion since the first part of December. We all hoped it would stay like that but we knew better. The peace talks in Manila weren't going very well and there was talk of a Tet truce as a bargaining chip for the talks. If this happened, we could count on heavy action.

The following morning we moved down from LZ Ruby into the surrounding Bong Son coastal plain area and began a methodical three platoon sweep of the surrounding hamlets. At the end of the day we would return to the LZ for the night. I liked the idea of being secure at night and having the entire company along with support artillery. It also meant a hot meal and mail.

Mail was probably the single most important thing to a grunt in the field. It was like a ray of sunshine or a glimmer of hope that we all so desperately needed. When one of your buddies drew a blank at mail call, the disappointment in his eyes told the story. It would be followed by a period of silence and if you got mail, you knew better than to flaunt it or say much. I was extremely fortunate that I had so many people writing me but some of the guys only got an occasional letter.

Steve "Doc" Vincent came up with a cure for the mail malady. Somehow, he had gotten hold of a list of potential pen pals in the States and he passed them around to anyone who was interested. This turned out to be a real morale builder. I picked a name off the list and I encouraged Mike to do the same. Mike was one of the guys who didn't get a lot of mail and I saw how it affected him. Mike went along with the idea and the three of us dashed off a short letter to our new pen pals. Now we all had something to look forward to.

I wouldn't want to say that I was glad to be back in country but I wouldn't want to be with any other group of guys. They were a perfect melting pot of the States. Each of them had completely different backgrounds and that always made for interesting conversation. Doc Vincent was a farm boy from Iowa. He was a husky kid with a big shock of curly red hair and an impish smile. He would tell me that I had a nice neck and he was looking forward to doing a tracheotomy on me. He had that kind of humor but he would be the first guy to lend a hand. He was a medic but when the chips were down he was right there with his M16. Doc liked to hang out with our squad. Sometimes he'd stay in one of our foxhole positions and he would share guard. He was an all around good guy and a competent medic.

We continued the sweeps in the valley but other than an occasional sniper, it was almost too quiet. We were hearing rumors that we might be deployed to Vung Tau as a security force. Vung Tau was a southern coastal town that was used for in-country R&R. That would be a good assignment but I had my doubts. Deep down I thought that these rumors were put out there for morale purposes and maybe that was a good thing. With another eight months to go in this hellhole, any kind of good news or rumors were readily accepted.

We received word that the battalion was being extracted from our present position and moved to LZ English for reassignment. Our hopes immediately jumped to the Vung Tau possibility. We were air lifted via Chinooks to LZ English. We were able to get a much needed cleanup and resupply. The Colonel addressed the battalion and told us that we would have a three day rest and then we would be spearheading a new operation called Pershing. This was not music to our ears. The Colonel was probably the only enthusiastic one regarding this mission. By now, we had him figured for a cowboy looking for medals, glory, and promotion. We just kissed Vung Tau goodbye.

The next three days were great; a chance to get some good solid rest and to share a few beers with buddies. There was a movie every night at English. It was like a drive-in without cars. You brought a couple of sodas or beers and sat on the ground under the stars and watched a flick. The movies that were shown were up to date and it was nice to have that little touch of home.

I took the time to catch up on my letter writing. Writing home was a good relaxant for me. It took me away from where I was and what I was doing. I had written Kathleen two letters and I had received none in response. It had been a month since her last letter. I sat there thinking about her and the fun that we had shared. There really was no commitment between us but I guess that I had made that assumption. I wondered why I hadn't heard from her.

The last time she wrote, she sent me a picture of her new Mercury Cyclone convertible. She had put an arrow symbol on the picture pointing to the 390 emblem on the fender. She loved fast cars and I could picture her flying down the highway with the wind blowing through her long dark hair. The car suited her to a tee. I suppose the notion of her sitting at home writing me letters for a year was presumptuous. How long would it be before some guy would see what I saw? I guess it was at that moment that I realized that I had gotten a "Dear John" without the letter.

That was two female downers in a row and not a good thing for my morale. I don't think the emotional damage was deliberate. The thing is that you are thirteen thousand miles from home and it's not like you can change anything. No one comprehends what it's like to be in a situation like combat unless they have experienced it. It was important for me to ponder the subject and get it put behind me but to dwell on it too much could be a dangerous distraction from the business at hand. Somehow I had to blind side it and keep going forward and keep my focus on the now.

I had managed to be very optimistic so far and I felt that it was the key to getting through all this. I liked to think that the meter was running and Vietnam was running out of time with every passing day. I knew that someday this would be behind me and I could go home and get on with my life. I was twenty-three years old and I had a lot to look forward to. I was a journeyman electrician and I had a great job waiting for me. I loved thinking about these things and it was a great depression deterrent. Most of the guys around me were three or four years younger than me and their futures were undetermined. Some were even married with no plans. I felt very fortunate that I didn't have those concerns.

Everyone was disappointed about starting another operation. This would be our third major operation. The fact that the battalion had come to Vietnam as a unit and joined the 7th Cavalry had special meaning. The other two sister battalions had seen heavy action in Ia Drang Valley and other places. All of the original 1/7 and 2/7 were gone and they had rotated into constant replacement status. We on the other hand were "fresh meat" and were going to get our fair share. In brigade's eyes, it was our turn. We spent a lot of our time talking about what the future might hold but in reality it was just conversation.

We spent a good part of a day cleaning our 81s and M60s. Sgt. Thomas, our new platoon sergeant, told us that when we deployed on Pershing, we wouldn't be taking the 81s. We would be operating as a fourth line platoon. Our load would be lighter but the danger would be greater. That bit of news didn't generate any cheer. We made sure that all of our normal weaponry was in top condition. An M60 machine gun would be in each squad as part of the fire team. All of us had been trained on the M60 but it would be assigned to a corporal or SP4. That didn't break my heart because that gun was the hottest and most dangerous job of all. The next day was our deployment day.

Evening came and a card game ensued. The players were Rich, Pete, and a new kid by the name of Willie. Willie was a big strong looking black kid from Mississippi. He had only been with us for a week or so. He loved to brag about everything imaginable. He was the best at everything. It was just a matter of time until Rich got a piece of him. Rich had gotten to me earlier and asked me to sit in on the game. I told him that I wasn't into cards. He handed me a bunch of MPC.

"You don't have to do nothing. All I want you to do is play until you lose that MPC and then you're out."

I looked at him and said, "What if I win?"

He came right back and said, "Yeah right. You got nothing to worry about. You're gonna win for a little while and I'm gonna lose. Willie's gonna think he's king and then I'm gonna take him down."

We were playing five card poker and Willie and me were winning. Rich and Pete were losing and Willie was busy shooting his mouth off about how nobody could whoop him. The game turned and I started to lose. Before long, I lost it all and I was out. A little while later, Pete was out and Willie was on a roll. He kept on bragging and Rich seemed like he was annoyed but I figured it was part of his poker face. For awhile, it continued to go Willie's way and he got more obnoxious with every winning hand. Rich looked over at Pete and me and gave us a wink and we knew that Willie's time had come. The noose was tightening.

Rich started to win hand after hand and before long had all his money back and was starting into Willie's. Within a half hour, Willie's money was gone and he was on the cuff. Willie's demeanor changed from the bragging jackass to the agitated asshole. Pete and I were enjoying watching Rich put this guy down hard. Willie was down two hundred bucks when he finally quit. Rich was giving him the needle like only he could do.

Willie told Rich, "I ain't payin' you shit, man."

Rich gave him a steely eyed look and said, "That so."

Rich turned and dug into his rucksack. He tossed a pad of paper and a pen to Willie.

Willie said, "What's this for?"

Rich replied in the most sinister voice I ever heard, "You write your momma a letter and tell her you won't be comin' back from Pershing. You're gonna be in a body bag."

They sat and stared at each other for what seemed to be a long time.

Willie jumped up and said, "You fu....g nuts, man!" He walked away.

Rich looked at us and said, "I'll get my money from that shit-head one way or the other."

About an hour later, I saw Willie and Sgt. Thompson walking toward our position.

I said to Rich, "Here comes trouble."

Sgt. Thompson was the first to speak and said, "Roderick, Willie just told me what went on down here. Now here's how it's goin' down. Willie's gonna pay you fifty bucks and there ain't gonna be no more gamblin' in my platoon. You got that! I don't like that threat that you made and I ain't gonna forget it. Nothin' better happen to him. Understand?"

He looked over at Willie and said "You gonna pay him dat money and you better learn to keep dat big mouth of yours shut. Dis ain't no game we playin' here."

CHAPTER 11

Operation Pershing

On 13 February 1967, Operation Pershing began. We were air assaulted into the north central section of Binh Dinh Province near Highway 1. We had been told that elements of the NVA 610th Division were active in this area and our mission was to find and destroy them. We all knew that the Tet truce was going to be a factor and that we had to be extra alert. There was no doubt that the enemy had been resupplied and that we would see more action.

My platoon was now a fourth line platoon. We would be CP security, reserve platoon, and heavy weapons. We had extra M60 machine guns and the whole company had been refitted with the latest weaponry. All of our grenadiers had M203s which replaced the M79 grenade launchers. These M203s were M16s that had a 40mm grenade launcher affixed to the underside of the barrel. The launcher could fire high explosive grenades and had an anti-personnel round that was the equivalent of a 40mm sawed off shotgun. The Captain and Lieutenants had the new Colt Commando M4s which were a shortened version of the M16 and had a telescoping stock. We were carrying lots of extra ammo and we all knew that the higher ups were expecting contact.

We were on the move every day and had light contact almost every day with units of squad size. We took prisoners and they verified that the 610th NVA Regiment was the main body of enemy in this area. This part of Binh Dinh was very familiar to us and we knew what to expect and where. We had gone up against the 610th before and we knew their tactics. They liked to attack or ambush late in the afternoon and be located near the tree covered foothills for escape. If they could inflict casualties at that time, their escape and evasion chances were good. They traveled light and could easily outdistance us in terrain that would give them cover from the air.

It was like a game of chase. We would make contact and kill a few of them and then they would disappear. The danger of a chase was that the enemy might be leading a unit into a trap. That's where Capt. Hitti excelled. He read the enemy well and used flanking maneuvers to herd the enemy into a position that was advantageous to us and support from artillery and air power. We had many factors in our favor. The important thing was to have leadership that knew how to use them to full advantage and that's just what we had. The leaders that we had were here to do a job, not for individual glory.

On the 18th of February, B Company made contact with a large force of well entrenched NVA. A fierce firefight ensued. Bullets were flying everywhere. I could see muzzle flashes to my front in a tree line. At that very moment, I heard a swishing noise just over my head followed by another to the left. I realized they were bullets flying by and that they had my name on them. I ran to my right and got behind a tree. Bark from the tree started to fly everywhere and I knew I was the target of a 30 caliber light machine gun. A squad from the 2nd platoon was scrambling to get an M60 set up to lay down a fire base so that we could maneuver. I poked my M16 around the side of the tree and dumped a clip in the direction of the tree line. I kept the firing as low to the ground as I could and continued to fire from both sides of the tree. Soon I heard the staccato chattering of the M60 and then another. There was smoke everywhere and screaming confusion.

Huey gunships were above the treetops and firing their rockets and machine guns into the tree line. The gunships pounded the

NVA positions until the artillery coordinates were radioed to a nearby artillery LZ. It went from the gunships to 105 and 155mm howitzers. Capt. Hitti was walking the artillery fire in the direction of the enemy escape route as we made our way to the tree line. The situation had changed and we were now in a slow pursuit through the trees. We had to be careful of the ambulatory enemy wounded as they could still shoot us as we passed them. There were bodies everywhere and the artillery barrage had shredded them in some cases beyond recognition. I tried not to look at the gore or to take mental pictures of the scene. We made our way through the carnage and stopped at a large clearing. We stayed concealed in the tree line as the company regrouped.

Our orders were to hold the line as battalion shifted companies into blocking positions. C and D companies had also made contact with the fleeing enemy. We learned that we had lost six troopers in the firefight and had several wounded. Bill Gould was one of the casualties. He was one of the guys that I came to Vietnam with from Ft. Polk. Bill was from New York and was a quiet guy with a good sense of humor. Sgt. Del Crockett had also been killed and I knew him as well. It's a very depressing thing to hear about these losses. It is another reminder of where we are and the reality of what we are doing. It is hard to comprehend the loss of someone. One day you see and talk to them and maybe the next day, they are gone forever. You just have to keep going. Looking around, many faces are no longer there.

The open area was secured and we received word that we would be setting up for the night. Positions were assigned and we dug in. Our KIAs and wounded would be medevaced from the clearing. Mike and I assisted with the bodies and loaded them on the dustoff choppers. Mike knew all six troops and he took it real hard. It is a grim assignment but I always kept it in my mind that we were sending these guys home as quickly as possible. That's all we could do for them.

Mike and I joined Doc Vincent at our position and made more preparations for a long vigilant night. As darkness fell, artillery fire missions began outside our perimeter. When the shells exploded, some of the free falling shrapnel was falling around us. If you got hit with a hunk of this, more than likely you would be cut and possibly burned because it was still red hot. Even though it posed some danger, it was very reassuring.

There was a C130 circling high above us and dropping parachute flares so that we could see. It was an eerie scene as the flares descended rocking back and forth in the wind and causing the shadows to move in sync. None of us were able to get much sleep and the night dragged on. We were expecting an early morning attack and we were pretty jumpy. This type of engagement from a singular position or even that of a squad was very uncertain. You couldn't see that many troops so it wasn't clear where everyone was or what your strength was. We had no idea of the size of the enemy force. Body count was an indication that it was a sizable force.

It was unusual for the enemy to make and maintain contact that early in the day. They no doubt had been resupplied and were more aggressive. Judging from their fortifications, they had been in the area for awhile.

This was the price of the truce. Our peace talk negotiators just didn't get it. The truce was what the enemy needed. The U.S. halts the bombing on the Ho Chi Minh Trail and the enemy resupplies its desperate troops in the south. The U.S. should have intensified the bombing of the Trail during the Tet and made the situation more critical and demoralizing for the enemy.

Zep made his way around the squad positions and told us what he knew and what we should do throughout the night. He and his RTO were in the center position about forty feet from us. He told us that our battalion CO, Col. Canham, had been severely wounded and that our former Lieutenant also was wounded. Maj. Bullock was now our battalion CO. Zep said that he'd probably hear more through the night and in the morning; he seemed very nervous and we took that as a bad sign.

The night finally came to an end and the sun was rising in the east. It was quiet to our front. We did some probing fire and there was no response. The intelligence and command choppers were circling above us.

Zep hustled over to us and said, "Saddle up. We're being rotated with A Company. The slicks (troop choppers) will be here in a half hour."

That was one order he didn't have to repeat. 1st platoon was the first to be lifted out followed by 3rd, 2nd, and 4th. We would be command and LZ security while the rotation took place. This would give Capt. Hitti time to brief Capt. Woods of the situation. The third wave of choppers arrived and the rotation was complete and we were in the air and on our way to the artillery position.

Gen. Westmoreland's Command Chopper at LZ Pony

When we got to the hilltop artillery position, we were assigned perimeter defense positions and each position in our platoon supplied one man each to assist the artillery with cleanup and resupply. They had expended tons of shells supporting us and today would probably bring more fire missions. I was assigned to the helipad to offload incoming choppers onto a mule (small flatbed transport) and the load would then be distributed to the guns. On the return trip, the mule would bring the expended cases. I don't believe I ever worked that hard. The choppers kept coming one after the other, unload and load.

A chopper came in that looked a little different. I slid the door open and all I saw was stars. Gen. Westmoreland, Maj. Gen. Norton, Brig. Gen. Moody, and Lt.Col. Gatsis hopped off the chopper. Gen. Westmoreland extended his hand to me and asked my name and where I was from. I responded and he asked where he might find Capt. Hitti. I directed them toward the CP and off they went. Later I would find out that Col. Gatsis was the new CO of our battalion. The battalion was in the midst of a fierce battle so there was no time for formalities. I had never seen that much brass at one time nor would I ever again. This was the third time that I had seen Gen. Westmoreland in the field. I saw him more than my division commanders. He was very much a field General.

After about a one hour meeting, the brass was back on the command chopper and in the air. We completed our job by early afternoon and I was dog tired. I returned to our position and Mike and Jim told me what they had heard. They said D Company had lost a platoon leader and Col. Canham had decided to land the command chopper and take command of the platoon. He spotted an enemy soldier and went after him. One of the gunships unaware of his position kept firing rockets.

The Colonel, his Lieutenant aide, and another trooper were wounded and one trooper was killed. The Colonel was badly wounded and needed immediate attention. Efforts were made to extract him but had to be aborted. They had become pinned down and needed help. Eventually elements of C Company were able to relieve them and get them extracted. None of us were surprised to hear the story. Later, we heard that the Colonel had lost part of his leg.

The battalion still had light contact with the 610th NVA and the fire missions continued. We were dug in along the side of the hill and the howitzers were above us. When they fired the concussion and roar was deafening. We could see the smoke below like a blue haze hanging above the tree canopy. By evening everything in the valley below was quiet and the guns were silent.

The next morning, we had a hot meal and it was our first in awhile. We had been eating out of cans and it was nice to have something hot and be able to eat it in peace.

There was a mail call. I got quite a few letters but none from Kathleen. I guessed that she was history. I did get a letter from my pen pal. I opened it in anticipation and could hardly wait to read what she had to say. Her name was Gloria and she lived in Huntington Beach, California. She said that she was glad to hear from me and that she looked forward to hearing back from me. Her letter was mostly questions about my situation. I wrote back and answered her questions and had a few of my own. I asked her to send me her picture in her next letter. I told Doc Vincent about the letter and he was pleased. He said Mike had gotten one too and I was real happy about that.

We got word that C Company had been extracted to LZ English and we would be following in a couple days. C Company had lost fourteen troopers in the firefight and they needed a rest. Post Tet February had been a tough month. The enemy had been renewed and we were paying the price.

Evening came and I went to get us some C rations and I noticed Zep, Pate, and Anderson sitting off by themselves. They had all their gear with them. I started to walk over to them to see what was going on and I was told by a senior NCO to stay away from them and to move along. I was totally confused and could not figure out what they had done to be isolated like that. It was obvious that they were shipping out and Zep was my squad leader.

I got the rations and went back to my position and told Mike and Jim what I had seen and been told. They didn't know what to make of it and we were coming up with all kinds of wild scenarios.

Mike jumped up and said, "I gotta find out" and away he went.

Mike retuned a short time later and said, "You're not gonna believe this but the word is that they re-upped to get out of here. Apparently the officers and senior NCO's don't want anyone talking to them. I had a hard time finding out that much about it."

We sat around talking about it and trying to figure out what was going to happen next. We would be needing a new squad leader and so would Pate's squad. Those three guys must have felt very fearful to do what they did. They were draftees and I'm sure they weren't looking to make the Army a career after what they had seen. They must have felt that they would be better off to do more time in the Army and to get out of combat while they still had the chance. The casualties were rising and maybe they wondered if they'd make it out alive and uninjured. I think those thoughts were on all our minds, even though we hadn't talked about it. It's a fear that we all tried to suppress. Who knows, maybe they were right.

Things were beginning to change too fast. Our platoon was falling apart. We needed reorganizing and some morale building. With our lieutenant and experienced platoon sergeant gone, we were in bad shape. All of us would have to step up and try to do more. As the turnover rate increased, experience, discipline, and confidence were declining. Up to this point, we had a great degree of optimism. We still had a long way to go and we had to get it together if we were going to make it.

We had a company meeting and Capt. Hitti eulogized our fallen comrades. One by one, he spoke of each trooper and their individual courage under fire. Capt. Hitti was an inspiration to us all. He was a courageous soldier with a lot of compassion for the men under his command. Listening to him, you could feel his emotion and loss. After he addressed the company, he had another meeting with the officers and NCOs. We were glad that the reorganizing process had begun.

The next morning, the company was airlifted by Chinook to LZ English for a cleanup and rest. This would give us the opportunity to try and put the week's events behind us. I was looking forward to a shower, clean clothes, a movie, and a couple beers. There was a big mail call and this gave me a chance to catch up on my letter writing.

I got a letter from my mother and she told me that my uncle Pat had to be put into a nursing home. I wasn't surprised because he had been diagnosed with Alzheimer's Disease before I went into the service. I could tell that she was very down so I wrote her right away and tried to be as conciliatory as I could. I was very fond of my uncle and I understood how my mother felt. I tried to be upbeat about my situation; I knew that would help her.

We had a platoon meeting and Sgt. Thompson went over the changes with us. He never said a word about the three NCOs that had just left. He made Randy the squad leader and Mike and Jim

Author waiting for air lift to LZ English

fire team leaders. I was happy with all his choices. He had definitely put some thought into it. There was no politics or ass kissing involved.

Randy came to me and told me that he had recommended me for fire team leader but that Sgt. Thompson overruled him. I told him what I thought and that it was fine with me. He said that he had something special in mind for me and that it would all work out. I thanked him and told him to do what was best for the squad. We all had the same goal and I could have cared less about rank. I think the choices that had been made had a positive effect on all of us and we needed that. That evening, we celebrated the promotions and took in a movie.

The next day, we were briefed about our next mission. We would be heading into the An Loa Valley again. Intelligence had information that the NVA 610th had fled into the valley. The terrain in the An Loa was thick with vegetation and was flanked by triple canopied massifs. It was an ideal place to be ambushed and hard to be ressupplied because the valley fingers were narrow. This wasn't going to be any cake walk. Bong Son was bad but An Loa was worse.

CHAPTER 12

An Loa Valley

It was the 1st of March and we were going to be making an air assault into the An Loa Valley. Everyone was as ready as they could be but we had a foreboding as to what was ahead. The enemy had been much more aggressive since Tet so we could only assume that they had gotten the manpower and supplies that they so desperately needed.

We were all on the helipad waiting for the slicks to transport us. I was on the second wave so it would be awhile before the slicks round tripped for us. I lit a cigarette to calm down. I was feeling very nervous about this assault. I didn't know why, I just did. Nobody was saying much and I'm sure they felt the same; call it a gut feeling.

I looked up at the cloudy grey sky and it had an ominous look to it. I could see the formation of helicopters coming toward us. They were descending quickly and there was a message to that. After awhile there were signs that could be read from the chopper take offs and landings. When they came in fast with the tail down, it usually meant the LZ was hot and the next wave was needed A.S.A.P. Another sure sign was if the crew chief jumped out and inspected the undercarriage of the chopper. He was looking for bullet holes or damage from hostile ground fire.

We boarded the slicks quickly and we lifted off immediately. The crew chief and door gunners were readying their M60s. There was no question in my mind about the LZ. Looking down on the terrain one thousand feet below, I could see rivers, hamlets, rice paddies, and mountains. In a strange sort of way, it was beautiful. The green was the greenest that I'd ever seen. The only spoiler was the huge round craters from previous B52 bombing runs. Seeing all these craters gave an idea of how much ordinance that had been dropped on this war torn land.

We were flying in a formation and I could see the faces of the troops in the slick next to ours. We were airborne for about ten minutes and I could see the massifs and the valley ahead. This wasn't our first time in here so I recognized the terrain. We started to descend and the slicks went into a single file formation. When we got down to one hundred feet the door gunner on the left side of the slick started firing bursts into the trees with his M60. I noticed the other slicks were doing the same. Randy gave me hand signals to head toward the opposite side of the valley when we off loaded. We would have to move fast in order to use the firepower of the slicks for cover as they lifted off. We hit the ground running and went for the cover of the tree line.

The slicks were lifting off and the gunships came in and strafed the tree line. This gave us the time we needed to join up with the first wave. We would hold this position until the third wave arrived. We joined our company and took positions in the friendly tree line. It would be our job to provide cover for the slicks when they returned.

There had been some harassing fire at us but nothing serious. A half hour later, the third wave arrived and we fired some base fire into the opposing tree line with no response. The gunships strafed the tree line while the third wave joined us.

It was beginning to rain and that put us at a disadvantage. It meant mud and misery. We crossed the valley toward the tree line and nothing happened. We started up the massif and it was rough going because of the mud. We were slipping and sliding as we climbed.

Huey air assault into An Loa Valley

On our way into battle

After an hour or so, we came upon an abandoned enemy encampment. The fires were still smoldering and the smell of Charlie was there. We found medical supplies and three dead NVA soldiers who had not survived their wounds. This encampment had all the signs of being a field hospital. We destroyed anything that was usable and continued our pursuit.

It was raining even harder now and leeches were dropping on us from the rain soaked vegetation. The worst part about leeches was knowing when they were on you. By the time you discovered them, they had sucked a lot of blood and were pretty big. They looked like a blood bag growing on the skin. I found that applying a drop or two of our mosquito repellant on them and they would drop right off. The other alternative was to back them out with a lit cigarette.

We were moving very slowly in three columns. This was a point man's nightmare. I couldn't help but wonder if we were heading into a trap. We struggled along for a couple of hours cussing the whole time. Between the relentless rain and slipping and sliding in the mud, it was miserable. Intelligence claimed that these tree covered massifs were the warehouses for the NVA's men, munitions, food, and hospitals. Our mission was to comb through this western massif finger and find them while C Company handled the eastern side.

We knew that we were right behind the enemy pushing him to the north. It was an exhausting pursuit and darkness was beginning to set in. It would be impossible to send out patrols or LP's under the canopy of the trees. Once it was totally dark, visibility would be at zero. We positioned ourselves behind trees and covered over with our ponchos. The smoking lamp was out. To light a cigarette would be a deadly giveaway of position.

The rain continued halfway through the night and we never had a chance to dry out before dark. We were cold to the point of shivering. I shook so hard that I only stopped from exhaustion and then after a few minutes it would start up again. Even breathing under the poncho didn't do much good because of condensation. It was the longest and most miserable night that I ever experienced.

The rising of the sun was a welcome sight. It would bring warmth and visibility. After a brief cup of coffee and some C rats, we were back at it again. There was no way that we could catch up with the enemy because of our load. The only way that contact would be made was on Charlie's terms and moving in column formation was not the way you'd want it. The point man and those right behind him were easy targets. It was a very tense situation and I couldn't remember a time when we moved so quietly. A couple hours into our second day, all hell broke loose in the distance. Small arms fire and grenades resounded across the valley. C Company had made heavy contact on the other side of the valley. Capt. Hitti was on the radio with the CO of C Company. He grabbed two platoons and started down the slope toward the valley below. We were instructed to continue in the same direction in case the enemy would try to flee in that direction.

I could hear all the communications over the radio as Capt. Hitti and 1st and 3rd platoons hurried to assist C Company. There were several casualties already. Our orders were changed. We were told to get down into the valley A.S.A.P. and prepare an LZ for medevac choppers. We moved as fast as we could down the slope slipping and sliding toward the valley below. 1st platoon was already in the valley and Capt. Hitti and 3rd platoon were on their way up the eastern slope to assist C Company. We got down into the valley and moved across where 1st platoon was located. We secured the area and made contact by radio with the medevac choppers that were now enroute. The small arms fire was still blazing up in the eastern massif and we were taking sniper fire on the LZ. The sniper fire was coming from the same direction that we had just come from. We had nearly missed being ambushed.

We fired at will toward the muzzle flashes in the trees and Lt. Foley called for an artillery fire mission at the western massif. The walking wounded from C Company began to appear on the LZ and Doc Vincent and another medic ran to their aid. I could hear the whopping sound of approaching choppers. The gunships came in first and strafed the western tree line where the sniper fire was coming from. The medevacs came in and one of our squads helped the wounded onto the choppers. We were securing the west side of the clearing. All firing had stopped on our side and Lt. Foley was pushing into the tree line with his platoon to see if there were any more snipers. He directed my squad to lend a hand with the evacuation of the dead and wounded.

We hustled over to the other side of the clearing and dropped our gear. Sgt. Thompson told me and Torres to collect and pile all the gear from the casualties so it could be loaded and shipped back to the forward base camp. There were eleven KIA's from C Company and somewhere around twenty-five wounded from C and B Companies. I was thankful for being on the equipment detail.

There were many severely wounded and they were the priority to evacuate. It was literally a bloody mess. I never got used to that sight. I had been in Nam for six months and B Company had lost over twenty men and well over a hundred wounded. When considering the time and numerical strength of the company, that was a lot. All you had to do was look around and there were many new faces. The company was turning over and only a handful of us were the experienced troops.

Mike spotted me and Torres and came over and told us that Capt. Hitti had been wounded and he saw him being evacuated. He said that he didn't think his wounds were too bad because he walked to the chopper by himself. This was really bad news. Capt. Hitti was a fine and capable officer and a true leader. We all knew that we would feel the loss of his leadership.

It was beginning to get dark and everything was mass confusion. Torres and I had finished on the LZ and we had no idea where anyone was located. It started to rain and total darkness had set in quickly. We made our way around the clearing looking for our platoon. There was an eerie kind of silence in the valley. We were cold and hungry. We saw a bombed out old French church with fires in and around the ruins. We made our way to it.

There were quite a few troops there but we didn't recognize anyone. We asked about our platoon but they said they were from C Company and had no idea were our guys were. It was obvious that they were in shock from the day's firefight and casualties. They were standing around the fires in silence trying to warm up. It was so strange with this church out in no man's land.

We decided that we would stay here until morning. We wanted to find a spot with some cover and away from the fires. As good as those fires looked, we didn't want to be silhouetted by them. It seemed like the troops that were by the fires didn't give a damn. Many of these guys had lost buddies and probably just didn't care.

Torres and I found a good spot to set up. It was a drainage ditch and there were some fallen trees that were nearby and they were big enough to use for cover if we were attacked. We got everything set up and decided how we would work the guard. I had a couple cans of fruit in my rucksack. I dug them out and flipped one over to Torres. We used our P38's to open the cans and marveled at how this little invention could open a can so quickly and easily.

We talked for a long while about what had gone on this day and how the loss of Capt. Hitti would affect us. He would be a real tough act to follow. We figured that Lt. Grady, our XO, probably would take command. Grady was an original officer to the battalion and seemed very competent. The main thing was that we got a good CO.

Torres was from Cuamo, Puerto Rico. He was a real nice guy, kind of quiet until you got to know him. He was a good trooper and always did what was expected of him. I liked having him around because I knew that I could trust him when the chips were down. We always spent a little time talking about home and our cars. He had a '62 Pontiac Catalina and I had a '61 so we had a car bond. He would tell me about Puerto Rico and all the pretty women. He told me that when we got out of this mess that I should come and spend some time there and we could have a lot of fun together. Torres was a good looking guy and I'd bet that he had a string of good looking chicks. I could just picture myself lying on some white sandy beach with a rum and coke in one hand and a hot Latino chick next to me. These were some great primal thoughts that helped get me through the moment.

The night passed slowly and there was no probing. The sun came up and the whopping sound of helicopters awakened me. Torres and I grabbed our gear and headed to the LZ. We ran into Doc Vincent and he told us where our platoon was and filled us in on what had taken place. The Doc always had the inside scoop on what was going on. He was our best source of information because he was linked to the other medics and they exchanged info. He told us that we would be getting a new CO in a couple of days and that it wasn't Lt. Grady. He also told us that he had talked to Capt. Hitti and that his wounds weren't life threatening and that he expected to come back to the battalion after his recovery.

We got back to our platoon and had a hot meal and a resupply of ammo, grenades, and C rations. Everyone in our platoon was okay. Our company had six wounded in the third platoon. C Company had taken the brunt of the casualties and they were extracted back to the firebase. We spent the day in the valley recuperating and waiting for battalion to decide our next move. We were all hoping that we would go somewhere else. An Loa Valley was a horrible place and a perfect place to be ambushed, mortared, and night probed.

It was March 4th and I realized that my mother's birthday was the next day. It was her sixtieth so I dashed off a letter to her and told her that I wished that I could have spent it with her. I loved to think about her and I could picture her laughing Irish eyes and hear her voice. She was a strong woman. I watched her pick up the pieces after my father's untimely death. She did what she had to do and she did it well. Any inner strength that I might have, I owe to her. I saw how she handled crisis and learned a lot from it. I finished the letter and got it in the mail sack for the evening log ship.

Word came down that we were going to sweep the valley and search and destroy. We would be moving out the next day heading north and deeper into An Loa. The good news was that we would be joined by two more battalions in an effort to flush the valley. I felt really good when I heard this. Usually when large scale offensives took place, the enemy went into hiding and our casualty rate went down. We were hoping for some quiet time.

The evening log ship came in with a nice hot meal and also our new CO. The new CO was Capt. Gibson. He was fresh from the states and had no combat experience. The Captain called a company meeting after chow. He told us a little about himself and what he expected from us. It was a typical pep talk. Let's go get 'em and kick ass. I don't think that he realized that he was talking to troopers that had been doing just that for the last seven months. He also spoke about medals and seeing to it that those who deserved them receive them. We had seen our fair share of heroes but I can honestly say that medals were not a topic of conversation among us. More often the discussion was about being safe and elapsed time of service or the three hundred-sixty-five day countdown. These were not war games that we were playing. The name of the game was to do your job and get back home in one piece. The winners were the survivors.

The next morning after a brief C ration breakfast, we moved out in a wide wing formation and started to move north toward an abandoned village about two klicks (kilometers) away. It was early but the sun was already pounding down on us and we were packing a lot of extra ammo. It was going to be a long hot day and a lot of sweating and cussing. Sweating was the body's way of cooling and a little mumbled cussing was good for the soul. It was a bit of a release from all the nonsense that you didn't agree with. We were the center rear platoon so we would be conducting the village search when we arrived. We knew what we were looking for so hopefully it would be uneventful. Point platoon moved through the village and the flanking platoons on the east and west held up while we moved into the village for the search under the direction of our new CO.

The village turned up nothing unusual. We checked the village water well because they were sometimes used for concealed tunnel entries. The Captain insisted on an extensive search of all the structures using bayonet wall probes and examining the floors inside all structures. He said that we were looking for weapon and supply caches. We knew better but it was a learning process for him and I'm sure he was trying to put some of the Vietnam schooling to use and to show us some of his leadership skills.

After a dozen or so of these hamlets, he would learn that the NVA and VC were much more sophisticated than that. He needed some time to get his feet on the ground and no doubt some of the lieutenants weren't too happy with his selection. The truth be told, I think an experienced lieutenant would have been far less disruptive than someone just arriving and being cast into a combat situation with no experience in country. Replacements and turnover would be a problem throughout the war and would create other problems. As all of this took place, the efficiency of the battalion was diminished.

We moved from village to village with the same results. After four days of this we entered a village that was located at the foot of one of the massifs. The village was occupied by women, children and old people. There were no males of combatant age. Sgt. Hung, our ARVN interpreter, questioned the villagers but no information of any value was gained. We moved across a huge rice paddy and into the next village where the CO decided to set up for the night.

Each platoon was to send a night patrol to a predetermined location and operate as a listening post. Randy grabbed me and four other guys for patrol. We would set out at darkness and return at first light. Randy briefed us on our mission. We were to cross the large rice paddy and go back to the village that we just came from and set up the LP there. We ate and prepared our weapons and waited for darkness.

We moved into the rice paddy and I observed that we had a full moon and I could see almost all the way to the trees that surrounded the village.

I said to Randy, "I think we are going to walk right into an ambush. Judging by the women in that village, their VC husbands probably come down from the massif at night. With this full moon, they can see us but we can't see them."

He came back with, "Yeah I know but the Captain insisted. He doesn't know the routine yet."

I said, "We better come up with a game plan so everyone knows what to do when the fun starts."

We decided to walk the dikes, two men on a dike and spaced ten feet apart. In the event of hostile fire, one man would go to the left and one to the right. By doing this we could use the dikes for cover and we would be able to maneuver. At least we wouldn't be bogged down in the middle of the muck filled rice paddy and we could keep our feet dry. I was carrying the PRC25 radio for Randy so I had to stay on top of him and go wherever he went.

We moved steadily trying to reach the intersecting dikes as quickly as we could. We got within two hundred yards of the village and still nothing happened. I felt like we were on a stage because of all the reflected moonlight.

Randy passed the word left and right, "Be ready. Get down at the first orange muzzle flash you see."

We got within one hundred yards when they opened up on us with small arms fire. We dove into the rice paddy and got down behind the dike.

I said to Randy, "You okay?'

He nodded and said, "Check the two guys on your side and I'll check the guys on my side."

I called to Torres and he said they were okay and Randy got the same response. The radio went off and it was the Captain calling for a situation report. I grabbed the mic and tried to get the antenna up and in doing it, an incoming round hit the dike in front of me and splattered mud all over my face.

Randy yelled at me, "F..k that radio. Get your ass down."

We were laying in about twelve inches of muddy water and about six inches of dung muck on the bottom. There was just enough room to keep our heads above water and behind the dike. Bullets were whizzing overhead. They had us pinned down and they could see any move we made. I handed Randy the mic and he requested mortar support. The Captain told him to attack the village.

"Is he out of his fu…n' mind? That would be fu…n' suicide.

Randy yelled into the mic, "Sir, we are pinned down by automatic weapons. We need mortar support and we need it now."

Our FDC (fire direction center) leader came over the radio.

He said "4/4, I have the village plotted and will fire one round of willy peter (white phosphor) for effect on your command."

Randy answered, "Fire one round for effect and I will adjust."

We heard the dull thump sound of the mortar tube and could hear the WP round whooshing toward its target. The explosion and white smoke was followed by a horrific screams and crying. The round had found its mark. Randy adjusted a HE (high explosive) fire mission in increments to the right and left of the marker round.

After the fire mission, there was an eerie silence from the village. We slowly got to our feet and proceeded toward the village. We got to the tree line and we could smell burnt flesh and heard the villagers crying. We were instructed not to go in until light and when the rest of the company arrived.

Randy looked at me shaking his head and said, "Can you imagine if we tried to charge that tree line? We all would've been killed. He's got a lot to learn. You were right about Charlie coming down at night. There were too many young women."

At first light, we could see the company crossing the rice paddy with the CO and his two RTO's out in front. Now if we could see him that easily so could Charlie. The company made it to the village and we all entered to find three smoldering dead VC bodies and a bunch of villagers wailing over them. No weapons were found. We figured there were at least a dozen shooters. The VC must have made their way back up into the mountains. This was more than likely a local militia.

Randy had really done a good job directing the men and mortar fire. If he had directed the mortar fire back into the village, there would have been civilian casualties. Even though these villagers were VC sympathizers, they were non combatants. Randy was going to make a good squad leader. He had good common sense and to show it under fire was proof. I felt good knowing that I'd be with him the rest of the way.

Steve "Doc" Vincent, Jim Haggerty, and Rich Roderick

CHAPTER 13

The School of Hard Knocks

The An Loa push was to last two more weeks. As I had suspected, operating with such a large force had reduced the combat action to minor scurmishes. We just went from village to village searching and destroying anything that was of military value. Whenever one of the units made contact, we were usually placed into a blocking position to stop an escape. The CO was itching for action but it just wasn't happening. At night, we were setting up in the closest village and sending out patrols. The patrols would usually go out about one to two klicks and set up ambushes along the trails leading to the village. LP's (listening posts) would also be set up to watch the dikes that crossed the rice paddies.

These night patrols were very scary because of the noise that we made as we moved. No matter how hard we tried or what precautions were taken, there was still too much noise. Charlie did most of his moving at night and he knew the terrain. He also carried little and his clothing was minimal. His movement was almost silent. This is where experience and common sense came into play. It was important to observe the terrain and who was in the villages. In short, you had to try to think like Charlie and figure out his motives for movement. The more experienced guys tried to educate the replacements as quick as possible because they would be with you on these patrols and your life depended on it.

B Company was way under strength. We had no platoon leader and we were short on NCO's. The CO was big into these night patrols and anyone with experience was leading these patrols. I had led some and it seemed as if I was being asked more and more. I could understand why because so many people were gone and experience was at a premium. It didn't matter how many of the night patrols that you took part in, it was a frightening experience. It was always in the back of your mind that you would run into a superior force and it would be "deja vous and Custer's Last Stand."

One night toward the end of March, I was told to take a patrol out and set up a listening post. Randy went over the location on the map and he let me pick the troops. I got four guys that I trusted and we made preparations to head out at darkness. We were instructed to set up near a main trail and watch and listen. Intelligence had reports that this trail was being used by enemy cadre and tax collectors.

We were to make no contact; just try to make an accurate enemy head count and direction if we spotted any activity. We started our mission in column with me on point and my RTO behind me and two flankers. The radio was off and we moved in silence. I could sense that everyone was nervous including myself. I figured the quicker that we could get to our destination, the safer we would be. It is better to be stationary than on the move at night.

We came upon a small hamlet with three small thatch huts. It was surrounded by a thick bamboo tree line. There was only one quiet way in and that was the main path. I decided to go in and take a look around and make sure that Charlie wasn't around. I wanted to make sure that the enemy wasn't behind us with the ability to cut us off from our main force. I went in first and instructed two men to go left and two to go right. I slowly made my way up to the center hut. There was an amber glow of light coming from the doorway of the hut. I could smell fish that had been recently cooked and there was a smoldering fire next to the door.

I used hand signals and we surrounded the hut. I made my way up to the doorway and I could hear female voices inside. I flicked the safety off my M16 and burst inside. There were three females inside. An old mamasan looked up at me with fear in her eyes and started to jabber in Vietnamese. There were two young girls with her. One girl was about ten and the other was about fifteen.

I looked around inside the one room and everything was okay. I smiled at the mamasan to show her that I meant no harm. I told two of the guys to check out the other huts. The old lady kept jabbering as she started to brush the teenager's hair. The teenager was very pretty. She had shoulder length black hair and beautiful white teeth. Teeth like those were rare in rural Vietnam because the women chewed betel nut and it turned their teeth purple. She was the most beautiful young girl that I had ever seen out in the bush or anywhere in Vietnam.

The teenager could speak a little English and I was able to tell her that we meant them no harm and we would be leaving shortly. I tried to ask about VC activity but the language barrier was too much.

She kept saying, "No VC. No VC."

What she was trying to tell me was that they weren't VC. I couldn't get through to her that I was asking if the VC were around or if she knew anything. As I tried talking to her, I couldn't get over how beautiful she was. She was very fine featured and was very developed for a Vietnamese girl. Her breasts were partially exposed and left nothing to the imagination and she made no attempt to cover them. Maybe she didn't realize it because most Vietnamese women that I ran across were very modest.

I told the guys to move out and the teenager gave us a faint smile and a wave as we left.

Leaving the hamlet, Jacobsen said, "Did you see the tits on that little bitch? She was beautiful. I'd sure like to bang her. I think she was looking for it and I haven't gotten laid in so long, I'm forgetting what it's like."

I said, "I don't think so and we have got to get to our LP and set up for the night."

Our LP was only a few hundred yards from the hamlet. We found a good spot to set up where we could see the trail and the entrance to the little hamlet. We could see the light from the hut from our position and we had good cover. I felt that it would be wise for us to keep an eye on the hamlet as well as the trail. I had the RTO turn the radio on and keep the volume as low as possible. He called in our first situation report and said that we were in position.

We were in position for about an hour when two of the guys came to me and told me that they were going to go back to the hamlet to bang the teenage girl. They wanted to know if I wanted in.

I said, "You're not going anywhere near that kid."

Jacobsen looked at me and said, "We're goin' whether you like it or not."

I snapped the safety off my M16.

"I don't think so. I'm in charge of this patrol and that ain't gonna happen. Understand?"

They both stood there looking at me for what seemed to be a long minute and then sat down a few feet away.

Jacobsen said, "We were just f.....g with ya. We wasn't really gonna do it. We just wanted to see what you'd say."

I looked up at them and said, "Yeah, right." I knew damn well they would have gone back to the hamlet and raped that little girl if I hadn't stopped them.

I told Freddie, my RTO, that I'd take the first watch and that we'd rotate the rest until first light. It turned out to be a quiet night. There was no activity on the trail. At first light we headed back toward the hamlet. When we got to the hamlet, mamasan and the young girl were outside the hamlet on one the dikes with their pants down around their ankles taking their morning constitutional.

This was a normal sight in rural Vietnam and more fertilizer for the rice. It was their plumbing and sewage system that had been in use for thousands of years. The simplistic and impoverished lifestyle of rural Vietnam was shocking to me. I don't think that I ever realized that there were people that still lived like this. They literally had nothing of any value.

As we made our way back to the company, Freddie said, "Aren't you worried about them guys wanting to get even with you? They were pissed at you. Don't you think they might try to frag you?"

I told him that I wasn't worried about two guys that would think about raping a child or any woman for that matter. I asked Freddie to forget about it. Sometimes shit just happens. Deep down I really hoped that they realized how wrong they were. Maybe we were kept out in the bush too long. The incident was never mentioned again.

We arrived back with the company just in time for the log ship with mail and a hot meal. I went through the chow line and got some scrambled eggs, sausage, and a canteen cup full of hot black coffee and searched out a shady spot to eat. It was about 6am and the sun was already blazing hot. I thought to myself, I had better fill my two canteens after I eat because this day was going to be a scorcher. Randy saw me sitting by myself and walked over and tossed three letters in my lap.

He stood there for a minute and said, "Something wrong, Powie? You're awful quiet."

I said everything was okay and that I was just tired. He turned and walked away and continued his mail run.

I read some of my mail and went into a little trance thinking about Kathleen and wondering what had happened to her. As hard as I tried, she kept popping into my thoughts. I thought we had a thing going on but I guess I was wrong. I wanted to write her but I was either too proud or too stubborn and I knew that I wouldn't do it anyway. Then Marge popped into my head and gave me another hollow feeling. I wished that things had worked out differently for us but they didn't. For some reason, I had women on my mind. Maybe the sight of the pretty little Vietnamese girl triggered these thoughts. It had been awhile since I had thought about them and I suppose it was just as well.

As I got to my last letter, I noticed that it was from California. It was from my pen pal in Huntington Beach that I had written. I read through the letter and it really made me feel good that a perfect stranger could take time out to write me. She enclosed a picture of herself and asked me if I had a picture of myself to send her. I could see from the picture that Gloria was very pretty. She was a gorgeous green eyed brunette.

She told me a little about herself and what she was planning for her future. She was a student at UCLA and had one more year to get her degree. Her degree would be in psychology and she hoped to find a job helping special needs children. I thought to myself, now here is a special person who is not only smart but cares about others. After I finished reading her letter, my whole mood changed. This letter was just the pick-me-up that I needed.

Randy called a squad meeting and tried to fill us in as best he could. He told me that he was happy with everyone and that he felt that I had been doing a good job. He was apologetic about asking me to go out on night patrol but he didn't have a choice. He told me that there was a lot of complaining about it but the CO didn't want to hear it. He said that he had told Sgt. Thomas to give me an allocation for SP4 and he figured that he would. I really didn't care much but if you're being asked to do the job of E4 or E5, you might as well have the extra money. In any event, I considered it a compliment.

The CO was on the horn with battalion and was receiving orders for our next movement. He called the platoon leaders and senior NCO's together for a meeting and the word filtered down that we would be moving out shortly. We were to move deeper into the An Loa Valley until we hooked up with the 5th Cavalry who were heading south. We would then be doing an about face and going right back the way we came in the hope that Charlie had come in behind us thinking that we would be air lifted out.

We started humping north and clearing all the villages along the way. We were able to move at a pretty decent speed because there weren't many inhabitants or villages in the valley. The rice paddies were pretty well dried up with no farmers to tend them or to keep the irrigation systems functioning.

It was a quiet run and we all appreciated that. I don't think our CO felt the same. He was itching for action and it wasn't happening. I think that a couple of these uneventful missions were sending him a false message about our enemy. Charlie picked his time and place. There was no doubt in my mind that the enemy intelligence on us was good and that they were probably very aware of our strength. There were scouts watching us and they were getting reports from sympathetic civilians on our movements. These civilians were recruited to do this or else by local and provincial cadre cells. The NVA and VC had learned a lot during the French Indochina War and were very well organized.

We met up with the 5th Cavalry in the center of the valley and then reversed direction and headed south toward our starting point. I expected that our return would be quiet as well. We were moving at a leisurely pace and the terrain was pretty flat. The only bad thing was the heat. I wondered what it would be like to live in a controlled environment again and to be able to maintain hygienic standards. I had never lived in squalor like this. It is amazing how a person can adapt to these types of conditions when you have no choice. As bad as it was, the enemy had it much worse. The odds of survival for them had to be horrific.

On the second day of our return mission, we were nearing the little hamlet where we had seen the pretty Vietnamese girl. We came upon some sort of open sided farm structure and we were struck with a horrible sight. Inside the structure lying on the dirt floor was the nude body of the teenage girl. It was very obvious that she had been raped. Her legs were spread apart and her clothing was ripped and thrown around. There was blood everywhere. She had been beaten badly and her throat had been cut from ear to ear. There were bite marks on her breasts. Her skin had turned a dark color and there were flies and maggots all over her bloating body. Her eyes were in the fixed stare of death. The sight was very upsetting to me. None of us had ever seen anything like this.

This was not a part of war. It shouldn't be like this. A few days before, she was a beautiful young girl and now she was dead and brutalized beyond belief. The Captain came over and took a look and just shook his head in disbelief. He told us to bury her. We dug a shallow grave and wrapped her in a poncho. We gently placed her in the grave and covered her with earth. Ironically it was Jacobsen and myself that buried the girl and I wondered what was going through his mind as we laid her to rest.

The guys found the old mamasan dead outside of the hut. She was lying in a pool of blood and her skull had been crushed. The little girl was huddled up in a corner crying. Sgt. Hung spoke to her and she told him that five VC soldiers had come looking for food. When they tried to force her sister to go with them, the old woman tried to stop them. One of them killed her with a blow from a rifle butt and then they dragged her sister off. She said that she could hear her sister screaming and crying for a long time and then everything was quiet. Sgt. Hung never told her what had happened to her sister. The Captain had a couple of the guys bury the old mamasan next to the young girl and we fashioned a couple of stick crosses to mark the graves.

The little girl was all alone and there were no relatives nearby so the CO decided to air evacuate her to LZ English and turn her over to the province chief for relocation. How very sad for the little girl. I wondered what would become of her. An atrocity like that stays with you forever. There is no way to block it from your memory. I was glad that she had not seen what had happened to her sister. It is hard to imagine that anyone could be that cruel to another human being. Even animals don't behave like that. I will remember it as long as I live.

We arrived back at our starting point in the valley with no opposition or incident. We stood on the LZ where it all had started waiting to be air lifted out. Everyone was quiet and probably reflecting on the past few weeks and all that had happened. It had been a depressing time and the ugliness and savagery of war had deeply affected all of us.

CHAPTER 14

Back to Bong Son

We were standing in the rain waiting to be picked up by chopper and air assaulted into the Bong Son Plain. The mission would be to seek out elements of the 22nd NVA Division that were known to be in the area. Once again, this was supposed to be a large scale operation and to me that was good news. It's like that old cliché, "There's safety in numbers." The higher the numbers were, the more support that was needed. The NVA knew that too so we were hoping for a good mission.

The terrain around Bong Son was more merciful than An Loa or Ia Drang and that would be a little relief. We would have to deal with more rice paddies but at least we would be away from the massifs for a while. I always felt most vulnerable when we were in a column with a point man maneuvering on these massifs. It brought our tactics down to the enemy level. They were at a definite advantage. Our mortars were useless because of the tree canopy. When you had open sky, any form of support was doable.

It was April now and we were moving into the hot season. It was hard to imagine it being hotter than it was but it would be. We were pretty seasoned to the adverse weather after over eight months but it still was nothing to feel good about. The rain would be a welcomed cool down.

The choppers came in and picked us up and we were on our way. We landed at LZ Ruby and it was a welcome sight. It was a fairly good sized artillery base and had several batteries. There were 105s, 155s and some 8 inchers. Ruby was also located pretty close to an ARVN airbase at Phu Cat. The ARVN's flew a lot of WWII aircraft on infantry support sorties. These aircraft were excellent for strafing and light bombing because of their short turning radius and their ability to dive bomb. Our fighter jets took miles to turn around for another pass. It was a good feeling to know that air support was so close by.

Once we were assembled at the LZ, we got a hot meal, mail, and an opportunity to clean up a little. We were pretty scruffy and it was nice to have a shave and wash up a bit. We would be leaving the LZ early in the morning and we had an opportunity to write a couple letters and get a little rest. The LZ was secured by another unit so there would be no patrols or guard.

I got to work on my backlog of letters. It seemed that I was always behind in my responses. There were probably ten of us sitting together writing away. Usually when we had a chance like this, it sparked a lot of personal conversation and took us all from the situation that we were in. Nobody wanted to talk about tomorrow. The rumor mill had subsided for most of us. It was what it was and there was nothing that we could do but deal with it.

I managed to get some sleep and the morning rolled around all too fast. We had a nice hot breakfast and a good cup of "Joe." The orders filtered down and we made our way down from the LZ to the flatlands below. It was the usual search and destroy mission and Sgt. Hung was to spend more time talking to villagers for intelligence information. We were going from village to village and staying in each for whatever time it took Hung and the S2 officer to do their questioning. It wasn't a bad job. Once we had done our village search, we could find a shady spot on the perimeter and wait until it was time to move on.

The CO picked a mangrove to set up in for the night. We dug our positions around the perimeter. I had two new troops with me and I gave them the rundown on guard and the do's and don'ts for perimeter security. I warned them of the night sounds of animals on the move. I explained that if they were convinced it was the enemy to use a grenade. I explained to them that the muzzle flash from their M16 would give away their position. We started guard at nightfall in two hour increments.

At midnight, I was awakened by two rounds of M16 fire from our position. I jumped up and crawled to our foxhole and found Gleason trembling and so shook up that he could hardly talk. I asked him what happened and he told me that he heard movement real close so he fired his rifle. He said he saw a VC in the muzzle flash so he fired again and he saw the VC falling and he didn't hear anything else. Truthfully, I didn't believe him. I figured it was the "new guy jitters." I told him to go back to where we had our hoochie and try and get some sleep. Randy came over and wanted to know about the rifle fire. I explained everything to him.

He said, "What do you think?"

"I think everything is okay and I haven't hearing anything.

I finished my watch and woke the other trooper to spell me. We went through our guard cycle and I wound up on the last shift that would bring in the daylight. It was a moonless cloudy night and visibility was zero. All you had was your ears for detection. I sat there staring out into the blackness. As the first light of day began, I saw something to my front. It was no more that fifteen yards away. It was a bare human foot. I grabbed my M16 and flipped the selector onto automatic and began to crawl to my front. As I got to the foot, I stood up with my M16 ready to blast. I looked down at the dead body of a VC. He had a grenade in his hand and his finger was in the ring of the detonator. He had been shot twice, once in the left side of his chest and once in the left thigh as he was falling. He was dead before the second shot hit him. The only clothing he had on was a pair of black shorts. His body skin had been covered with black camouflage grease. The grenade was his only weapon. He must have watched us dig our foxhole and set up our hooch and then slowly crept toward our position.

He was probably seconds away from pulling the pin on that grenade and dumping it in the foxhole when Gleason fired. According to the book, Gleason did the wrong thing by firing his rifle but there was no doubt that it saved his life.

I went back and woke the two troops and brought them up and showed them the body.

Gleason looked at me and said, "I told you I saw him."

There wasn't much I could say except, "Good shooting."

Everyone in the company came down to look at the sight and it was a good wake up call that we were being watched and now probed. We all had to be as sharp as possible. It was easy to get complacent when everything was going okay. It took something like this to bring us back to reality.

We spent the next week doing the same type of operation. Intelligence had gained a lot of information and was trying to piece it together. This would determine our next mission and whether we would continue to operate in this area. Before we received an answer, we were told that one of our recon units had made heavy contact in the An Loa Valley near the village of Hung Long. We were told to prepare for an immediate air assault. We were briefed by our platoon sergeant and told that we were being placed in a blocking position to cut the enemy off from a possible escape route.

We air assaulted into the An Loa Valley east of the Song Bao River which was a small tributary of the Song An Loa River. The LZ was cold and the fighting was all west of the Song Bao. We were at the base of a massif which would be a natural escape route for the enemy. If the enemy could avoid contact with us and make it to the massif, he could easily escape.

The CO got on the radio and requested permission from battalion to cross the Song Bao and assist the unit under fire. Battalion gave him permission and he led three platoons across the river. 4th platoon was their cover while they crossed the river and was to remain in blocking position on the east side of the river. Almost immediately after crossing the river, the three platoons came under heavy small arms fire. We could see tracers flying every direction in the tree line across the river.

We got orders from the CO to cross the river. We spread out and waded into the river. We knew that we had to cross as quickly as possible or we might be trapped in the river with no where to go. I can't swim so I was particularly nervous about the crossing. The water kept getting deeper and deeper and I had my M16 over my head. Jim Pitzen was in front of me and I was trying to follow him. By now the water was up to our necks. All of a sudden Jim went under and didn't come up. I moved forward a couple of steps and crouched down and groped for him . I felt his shoulder and grasped his collar. I used my legs and pulled him up with all the strength I could muster. He was spitting out some muddy water but he was okay. He said that he stepped in a hole and went under on his knees and he couldn't get up. He thanked me for helping him. We made it the rest of the way okay and we regrouped by squad and started toward the tree line.

The shooting had stopped and we were trying to hook up with the rest of the company. We had no idea where they were exactly. We were in column walking along a long row of hedges. I happened to look down into the hedgerow and there was one of our troopers with his rifle pointed in our direction.

He looked up at me and said, "You better get the f..k outta there. They're right on your left in that hedgerow over there."

We moved quickly around behind the hedgerow and found whatever cover we could and got down in the prone position. Why the enemy didn't open up on us, I'll never know. We had walked right between the two forces. We weren't there five minutes and it all started up again. Bullets were flying everywhere and we couldn't shoot because we were behind our own men.

We had no fix on where the other two platoons were so we didn't know what we could do to help. All we could do was stay put until we got some direction. The firefight lasted for about a half hour and then the all firing came to a sudden halt. In a matter of minutes, things went from bedlam to silence. No one was moving. I was with Haggerty and Willie and we were maintaining silence and looking around for direction or some activity that would signal a move for us.

It was beginning to get dark. We were in an open area that was ringed by hedgerows and we were in the prone position by the roots of one of the rows. It really wasn't cover but more of a blind. I looked across the open area and I saw a small group of troopers. I recognized Randy and two other squad leaders. Jim said he'd work his way over to them and find out what was happening. Jim got up and made his way across the clearing and Willie and I covered him.

When Jim returned, it was completely dark. He told us that Capt. Gibson was missing along with his RTO's. He was last seen advancing through an opening in the hedgerow. There were four KIA's and several wounded. He said that one of the new troops had gotten scared and tossed a grenade over a nearby hedgerow and had wounded three of our medics. One of the medics was Steve Vincent, our platoon medic and part of our little group. Steve would be a big loss to us and our morale. Jim didn't know how badly he was wounded but past experience told us that he was gone for good.

There were medevac choppers on the way to remove the dead and wounded. Jim said we were to maintain our position and that the rest of the company would be positioned around the perimeter hedgerows to secure the open area that would be used as an LZ. The medevacs would be brought in by radio and flashlight. As soon as this was accomplished, artillery would ring us with H&I fire.

We did our best to improve our position and gain some cover without making any more noise than necessary. The situation was very uncertain and there was no doubt that it was going to be a long night. The medevacs arrived and created an eerie sight. The running lights on the choppers and the flashlights of those who guided them in were all that we could see. As soon as the dustoff was completed, the artillery fire commenced. We were being ringed by fire and as the HE rounds exploded around us, we could feel the concussion through the ground. The large hot chards of shrapnel were whooshing through the air and free falling to the ground with a loud thud. The shrapnel was falling all around us. We figured that these rounds were coming from 8 inch howitzers.

We also had support from 'Puff the Dragon' which was a DC-3 aircraft that was fitted with three gattling guns which were capable of firing six thousand rounds a minute. When these machine guns were fired they sounded like the roar of a dragon and the red fire from the tracer rounds was a solid red line to the target. They also carried flares that could produce two hundred thousand candlepower of light. The flares were attached to mini parachutes and made an eerie squeaking sound as they descended. The flares lit the terrain but also lit us up. The fact that we didn't have much cover gave us a feeling of nakedness and vulnerability.

It was another long and uncertain night. We had little knowledge of what was going on or what we were up against. We would just have to wait for daylight and hope for the best. Now with Doc Vincent wounded and gone, our main information link was gone.

With the first light and the Captain missing, I expected an attack, confusion, and chaos. I was completely wrong. There was a somber quiet air but organized. Lt. Sipple had unofficially taken charge and he seemed to have a handle on the situation. Apparently the enemy had retreated under the cover of darkness and everything was quiet. Lt. Sipple sent out two patrols out to see if they could locate Capt. Gibson and his RTO's. The rest of us were to hold our positions until the patrols returned with a situation report on the enemy and our missing troops.

No more than a half hour went by and one of the NCO's came and got six of us and told us to follow him with just our rifles. We crossed through the next hedgerow and went about thirty more yards and there were the bodies of the Capt. Gibson and his RTO's. They had been killed by small arms fire and they had been hit several times. It was apparent that they had died instantly. It was a gruesome sight. There was a lot of blood and I've always been on the squeamish side when it comes to that. I had not been chosen for body recovery in a while and it made me a little nauseous. I knew that I could never get used to this no matter how many times that I did it.

We wrapped the bodies in ponchos and carried them back to the secured open area. The patrol that found the bodies brought all the weapons and gear that belonged to the fallen troops. We laid the bodies down and made sure that they were completely covered. One of the lieutenants went through their gear and separated personal effects from military and called for a dustoff.

We returned to our position to await further instructions from our squad leader, Randy. We were very quiet and really didn't say much to one another. It had been a bad day for B Company. We had lost our company commander and six NCO's. There were eleven wounded and three of them were medics including our own, Steve Vincent. I had a sick feeling in my stomach and was having a hard time realizing that these guys were gone. This time it was different for me because I knew some of these guys personally. There is a lot of truth in that old combat cliché, "Don't get too familiar with those around you." Of course, that is a whole lot easier said than done.

Capt. Gibson had a large family and now his children would grow up without a father. Someone said that his wife was expecting. What a tragedy for his family. This is the part of war that no one thinks about, the terrible loss to the families of the fallen.

Four of the six NCO's that were killed, were experienced and original members of the battalion. Their loss would be greatly felt. Every fire fight was causing us to lose more and more key people. We were undermanned in almost every position and the lack of experience was becoming a major problem. The company was now desperately in need of replacements.

The dustoff choppers arrived and we watched as the bodies of Capt. Gibson and the other fallen troops were being loaded for transport to LZ English and on to Saigon. A strange and empty feeling came over me as I watched the chopper lift off and bank to the south as it climbed into the morning sky. The same thought that I had so many times before was on my mind again, one day you are here and in just a few moments your life is ended. It is almost as if these men never existed. I couldn't help but wonder when it would be my time or would I be lucky enough to make it out of this hell-hole. As hard as I tried, I couldn't keep these thoughts out of my head.

Randy came and grouped the squad together and told us that we would be staying in this area long enough to police it for enemy bodies, weapons, and equipment. A bulldozer and some engineers from the 8th Eng. Battalion would be flown in to bury the NVA bodies and to destroy any enemy fortifications. After that was completed, we would be air lifted to LZ Dog in the northern coastal region of Binh Dinh Province for reorganization and a little recuperation.

Looking down at the Song Bao River from a huey

CHAPTER 15

Binh Dinh – Coastal Plain

As we lifted off the battlefield on our way to LZ Dog, I looked down at the Song Bao River and the hedgerows. I knew that I would always remember the events that had taken place here and the men that were lost and wounded. I couldn't help but wonder what had been accomplished. It seemed like we were spinning our wheels, coming and going to these same places and never pacifying them. The terrain of Vietnam made that impossible. Until the enemy decided to throw in the towel, it would remain like this. The determination and staying power of the enemy was something to be respected.

The choppers came into LZ Dog and touched down in a huge cloud of red dust. The dust was in our eyes, mouths, and clothes. I could taste the dirt and I felt dirty and tired. I was hoping to clean up and have some decent food and most of all some precious sleep.

LZ Dog was a large artillery firebase located on a barren hill-top in the northeastern region of Binh Dinh Province on the Bong Son Plain. It took a full strength infantry company to secure its perimeter. B Company was so under strength that we needed a platoon from a sister company in order to man the perimeter. We would be getting replacements while we were here and probably a new company commander. The main thing was that we would get a rest and try to put some of our hardships behind us.

Randy assigned us to our positions on the perimeter and we drew a northern side position and down a little from the crest of the hill. We were set up below a battery of 105's on a hillside. If there could be any hope of shade from the blistering sun, it would be here in the afternoon. I had Torres with me and I felt good about that. He was a little nervous but very alert and I knew that my back was covered. Torres took Vietnam very seriously, his main objective was to do his job and return home safely. We were on the same page with our objectives.

I felt good about being at LZ Dog because it was pretty close to Highway 1. There was a lot of security along this road as it was the main artery going north and south. Highway 1 was secured by the Korean Tiger Division, one of Korea's best combat units. These troops didn't mess around. They loved to put on demonstrations of their martial art skills in all the villages up and down the highway. It was their way of telling the people that they could be tough and should be respected. It seemed to work because the VC left them alone most of the time.

We heard that one of their positions had been attacked at night and that three soldiers had been killed and others wounded. The next morning, a Tiger armor unit mounted a retaliatory attack in the surrounding area. They returned a few days later with several bodies dragging from ropes behind their armored personnel carriers. When they arrived at the nearest village, they cut the bodies loose in the middle of the road. The bodies had been dragged for several miles and were horribly mutilated. This was their response to the attack; don't f..k with us.

Another thing they would do was fire their 50 caliber machine guns at night. If we were anywhere near Highway 1, we could hear the chattering of the guns and see the red tracers flying every which way. I don't think they were overly concerned about what they were shooting at. This must have been   another one of their deterrents from night probes.

We stayed on LZ security for a few days and then the brass decided to ship us back to Camp Radcliff for a cleanup and rest. A company from another battalion came in on choppers to replace us and we boarded the same choppers and headed for Radcliff. It was a good feeling to be going back to our base camp. I knew there would be new clothing and a hot shower and we all desperately needed both.

We lifted off from LZ Dog and as we ascended, I watched the LZ disappear below. There were no doors on the choppers so flying was very exhilarating. The wind blowing through the chopper was refreshing. For the first time in quite a while, I felt good. I guess it was just uplifting to know that we were out of action for awhile.

We were in flight for short time and I could see Camp Radcliff to our front. I could see the Golf Course (airfield) and Hon Cong Mountain with our division insignia on top. We descended down into the camp and landed on the main road in a single column. As we hopped off the choppers, the division band was along side of the road and playing the "Song of Garry Owen." They were dressed in the old uniforms of the cavalry, the dark blue with yellow bandanas, riding boots and the big Stetson hats with the crossed sabers. It was quite an honor to have the band playing for our return.

Once the battalion was all assembled, we were marched by several 55 gallon drums filled with ice cold beer and we were each given two cans. Then we were herded into a fenced-in area and told to remove our personal effects from our clothing and to place them with our rifles and our gear. We were told to remove all our clothing and to throw them into a fire pit. Now here we were, standing buck naked and drinking two cans of beer while a bunch of Vietnamese women on the other side of the fence were laughing and quite amused by our situation. We must have been quite a sight to them but none of us cared one damn bit.

Next came hot showers with bar soap and hair shampoo. When the water hit our filthy hair, red dirt ran down our faces. I will always remember that shower and what it felt like to be clean again. After the shower we were issued new jungle fatigues and socks. We got dressed and walked down the road to our battalion area. It's strange how something like that can mean so much and make you feel so good. I guess we never really appreciate what we have until it is taken away. I found out what it was like to have nothing and I would remember it forever.

We had a nice hot meal in the mess hall and for the first time since I returned from R&R, I was able to sit down at a table with my buddies and enjoy it. The food was good and I think that a special effort had been made by the cooks because of our losses. We even had ice cream for desert.

When we were done, we went outside for mail call. I got a couple letters and one was from my mother. I opened it and began to read it and there was bad news. My Uncle Pat had passed away. That hit me hard. He was very special to me. He looked after us after my father's death. He would walk over to my mother's house every Saturday to see if everything was okay and to see if we needed anything. He would always leave a fifty cent piece on top of the television for me and my brother. He and my Uncle John were like second fathers to me.

Uncle Pat was failing with Alzheimer's Disease before I left for Vietnam so I knew his demise was coming. I remembered going to his house to visit him.

He said to me, "Why the hell are they sending you young kids over there. They should send me because I'm old and my life is just about over."

I could picture him with his LaPalina cigars and laughing after one of his many jokes or impersonations. I looked up at the sky and said goodbye and a tear ran down my face.

Randy and Mike spotted me sitting off by myself and they could see that I was upset. They asked what was wrong and I told them. They sat down with me and got me talking and they were kind enough to listen to me rattle on. Talking about it helped me get that emotion out and I felt better.

Mike said to me, "You were lucky to have an uncle like him."

Randy chimed in and said, "On a lighter note, you've been promoted to SP4 and we're all getting the Air Medal for air assaulting into hot LZ's"

Four days later, we were back out in the boonies again with our new CO. His name was Capt. Manthey. He seemed like a real nice guy. He was on his second tour in Nam and he wasn't too happy about it. He called the company together for a meeting and told us what he expected of us. He said that he believed in tight perimeters at night and that he wouldn't be volunteering us for unnecessary missions.

He also wasn't big into night patrols. He said that he had learned from his previous tour that it was too dangerous and the rewards weren't worth the danger. He felt that we were at a great disadvantage in not knowing the terrain and how to maneuver it as our enemy. This was music to our ears. Now we had a combat experienced commander who was not gung ho. Here was a guy just like us who wanted to do his job but wanted to go home in one piece. He wasn't looking for medals or rank.

We were back to our search and destroy mode on the coastal plain area of Binh Dinh Province. This was the far north region along the border of I Corps. S2 had reports that elements of the 22nd NVA and the 2nd VC regiment were operating here. We were near Gia An when we made contact and a firefight ensued. We were getting lots of small arms fire from a small hamlet on our flank. The CO quickly repositioned the platoons and established a fire base of M60 machine gun fire. The mortar platoon set up a gun and started to drop WP rounds for markers and followed that with HE rounds. It ended almost as quickly as it had started. The enemy fire from the village had ceased so our leaders called a cease fire.

Based on the amount of fire caming from the hamlet, we had met up with a sizable unit and they were fleeing north. B Company had one trooper killed and three wounded. The CO took two platoons and entered the hamlet only to find it abandoned. There were several enemy dead but their weapons were gone. They were uniformed NVA Regulars.

The medics tended the wounded and called for a dustoff. The company couldn't go into a full pursuit because of the wounded. Our sister Companies, A, C, and D, went into pursuit. We were to hook up with them as soon as the dustoff was completed. It was a half hour before the medevac arrived and darkness was setting in quickly. The CO decided to set up in the hamlet for the night. We secured the perimeter of the hamlet. I had two guys in my position and we were on the north side of the hamlet. We would be especially alert in case there were any enemy stragglers who might be headed back in our direction.

Randy came by and told us that our sister companies had trapped the fleeing enemy in a village just north of us. An armored tank company was being sent down to assist and the battalion was going to attack in the morning. When the armor reached us we would follow them to the besieged village and join in the attack. I had never been around any tanks but it was comforting to know that we would be behind them as we attacked.

The night passed quickly and everyone was apprehensive about the morning. Typical of soldiers, we were reading the worst into it. We figured if the brass was bringing a tank company in, they must anticipate a helluva fight. We went over every possible scenario and none of them were good. We had all night to think about it and that's just what we did.

First light came and we started to prepare for the attack. We checked all weapons and made sure that we all had our standard issue of ammo. A log ship arrived and dropped off mortar rounds, M60 and M16 ammo, and medical supplies.

Our sister companies had the village surrounded and other units had been placed in blocking positions. We were to approach the village from the south following the tanks and fight our way in. Everyone seemed a little jumpy. I thought it was probably because of the tanks or too much information. Sometimes you're better off if you know less. The more time spent thinking about something, the more fear. This was one of those times. Most of the time our contact with the enemy was spontaneous and there was no time to think, just react.

There was a rumbling sound in the distance and we spotted three M48 tanks heading toward us. It was a very impressive sight and soon we could actually feel the vibration through the ground. The tanks rolled up to the hamlet and the tank commanders dismounted.

Capt. Manthey walked over to them and they set up a plan of attack. He assigned each tank a platoon of infantry and held the second platoon in reserve for reserve support. We moved into our position behind the tanks. We were ready to go.

The tanks started to move at a walking speed and we proceeded across a large open area in the direction of the surrounded village. There was no gunfire coming from the village. We got within a hundred yards and we figured that the firefight would begin. I have to say, it was a great feeling having that fifty-two ton steel monster in front of us. It had a 105mm. main gun, a 50 cal. turret machine gun, and a 7.62mm. machine gun.

We were approaching the village and still there was no gunfire. The three tanks came to a halt and one of the tank commanders climbed down from his turret and walked to the front of the tank. He walked a little further toward a large water filled irrigation ditch. My squad escorted the CO up to the ditch to talk to the TC. The TC told Capt. Manthey that the tanks couldn't cross the ditch and that if they tried they would get stuck in the ditch. He said that they would have to go to the main entrance to the village and enter that way. The village was pretty good sized and it would take them awhile to enter from the east. The CO got on the radio to battalion and explained the situation. Battalion ordered us to move forward without the tanks, cross the ditch and attack.

The tanks rumbled off to the east and we moved forward across the ditch. The water in the ditch was about two feet deep and there was a foot of muck on the bottom and it was loaded with leeches. We had our pant legs bloused onto the top of our boots and hopefully that would stop the leeches from going up our pant legs.

We crossed the ditch and climbed up the embankment on the other side in full view of the village and still nothing. This would have been the perfect opportunity for the enemy to open up on us.

We made out way to the bamboo berm line that surrounded the village. We hacked our way through the thick undergrowth with machetes. We got through and still there was nothing. It was pretty apparent at that time that our enemy had some how eluded us. The tanks had now entered the village from the east and were smashing their way through some of the huts. We went into search mode looking for any indication of how the enemy escaped or if he had been forced to leave anyone or anything behind.

We found about twenty dead NVA soldiers who had been killed by the preemptive strikes. We worked our way to the northern side of the village and one of the M48's fired a 105mm. round to the north. The round struck a tree and exploded and the fragmentation hit Capt. Swain, D Co. CO, in the head mortally wounding him and wounding an artillery lieutenant. Capt. Swain's company was in a blocking position to the north of the village. They weren't under fire at the time and it wasn't clear why the tank fired the round from the village in their direction. I don't recall any hostile fire on that day.

Capt. Swain had been battalion S2 officer prior to taking command of D Company. I remember seeing him in that capacity many times in my first six months. All the original members from Fort Carson spoke very highly of him and felt that he would go a long way in the Army. He was on his second tour. It was a sad day for the battalion and to lose a capable leader to friendly fire made it even worse.

We had thought this was going to be a big battle and with us being the attackers, the casualties would be high. The direct opposite was the case. Nobody would have anticipated this outcome. This was the first and last encounter that I would have with armor while I was in Nam. I guess all that could be said was this wasn't the right terrain for armor. That wasn't much consolation for Capt. Swain's family.

Willie and Torres

CHAPTER 16

A Friend Lost

It was the 1st of May and I was beginning my ninth month in Nam. The previous eight months were terrible and I was hoping that we would get some sort of reprieve. My lower back was bothering me a lot and I had taken on a slight limp. The pain was almost a daily thing. Whenever we got back to LZ English or Camp Radcliff, I would go to 15th Med. and get this checked out. In the field, there was nothing that could be done. There was no such thing as a pain killer. The last thing a guy needed here was to be half out of it. As hard as it was sometimes, you had to stay focused.

The battalion was still operating in Binh Dinh Province around Binh Duong. We were still trying to eliminate fragments of the 22nd NVA Div. which had so skillfully eluded us the week before. The contact was mostly hit and run and some sniper fire.

The weather had taken a turn for the worse. It seemed like every day was hot now and not a lot of rain. Our water consumption was greater and it took a lot more stamina to hump the area with a sixty plus pound load on your back. We all had white salt stains on our clothing from sweat and there was no way to control our own stench. I will always say the physical anguish of Vietnam was almost as bad as the combat. It seemed like there was misery in one form or the other every day.

One of our platoons was acting as lead when automatic fire suddenly came from a tree line on their flank. One trooper was killed immediately and two others wounded before they could take cover. The Captain dispatched a platoon to flank the enemy position and set up a base of fire. Weapons platoon set up an 81mm. mortar and dumped six rounds of high explosive down the enemy's throat. When it was over we found eleven dead NVA and another six critically wounded. The rest were able to get away before we could call in air support but it seemed as if we were moving in the right direction. We had to hold our position and evacuate the wounded and the wounded prisoners. The CO selected a temporary LZ and called for the dustoff. By the time the choppers arrived, four of the wounded prisoners had died.

The company continued to search the hamlets without finding anything of military value. The villagers in the area were heavy VC sympathizers so we didn't gain much intelligence from them. We continued the routine moves of search by day and set up tight perimeters at night.

On the 3rd of May, we set up our night perimeter and I was with Torres and Haggerty. We had a good position with a good field of fire and the best news was there was an irrigation ditch about twenty feet long. This meant that we wouldn't have to do any digging. The ditch was even the right depth. We set up a two- man hooch for sleeping. I couldn't have had two better guys with me. We had more and more replacements coming in and it was unnerving if you wound up with two "newbies". There was always the fear that you could be probed at night and be either overrun or fragged. This area around Binh Duong was a likely spot for that scenario.

A log ship arrived with some C rations and mail. We got our portions and sat on the edge of the ditch and ate our C's and read our mail. We talked and swapped stories of home, cars, and girlfriends. Torres always had some great stories of wild beach parties and good looking women. I totally believed him because he was a good looking kid. He had a big flashy smile and an easy going way about him. Haggerty was a great guy as well. We would listen to Torres and both of us would be laughing at his stories.

I had first guard watch, followed by Haggerty and then Torres. We would start on the hour at darkness. I sat on the edge of the ditch staring into the black silence to my front. It was a moonless night and I couldn't see my hand in front of my face. It was nights like this that you had to totally rely on hearing. There were small animals roaming at night and they could easily be confused with enemy movement. I appreciated the fact that we didn't have to dig our position. I felt that Charlie could watch you dig your position and study the terrain to your front and worst of all he knew right where you were. In this situation, I felt like we had the advantage. We weren't moving and neither could see each other. Charlie had no way of knowing exactly where we were.

During these guard hours, I liked to think of home. My mind would cover a myriad of subjects. It's something how thoughts about the past would come to mind when you're staring and listening for two hours. This made the time go by quick for me.

Before long my time was up and I went and awakened Haggerty. I gave him a brief situation report and then I laid down next to Torres and hoped that I could get a few hours of sleep before my next watch. I got lucky and went into a deep sleep.

It seemed like a short time had elapsed and there was an explosion. I sat up and I felt someone sit up next to me. It was Haggerty.

I whispered to him, "What the hell was that?"

I called softly to Torres and there was no response. I tried again and nothing.

I whispered to Haggerty, "You go to your right about ten yards and I'll go to my left and we'll crawl toward the ditch. When we get there, we'll drop in and make our way to the middle."

He agreed and we grabbed our rifles and started to move. There was no sound to our front or where Torres should have been. I crawled slow and steady, stopping to listen every five feet or so. I got to the ditch and dropped in feet first and in a crouching position, I made my way to the center. Haggerty got there first.

He called softly to me, "I found him, Bob. He's dead. He's torn apart. It must have been a grenade."

Before we could say anything else, I heard Randy's voice calling to us. I stood up.

Randy said, "What's goin' on?"

I said, "I'm not sure. Torres is dead and we think it was a grenade. We don't know whose grenade."

Haggerty was so upset that he could hardly speak. He and Torres had been together since they came from Tigerland. I was pretty upset myself because I liked Torres and it is especially hard when you lose someone you know real well. We had all been together for seven months.

Randy said, "C'mon outta the ditch. I'm gonna get some other guys down here."

We moved about ten feet back from the ditch and sat down next to each other.

Randy said, "I'll be right back."

He turned and moved quickly toward the company CP. Both of us were speechless and didn't know what to say. What had happened? Torres was so careful. Was it an enemy probe or a mistake? We both just sat there with tears in our eyes staring out into the darkness.

A few minutes passed and Randy returned with Capt. Manthey, Sgt. Marcano, and a couple guys from one of the other platoons. The Captain questioned us and asked us what we thought and we both told him that we thought it was a hit and run probe. Capt. Manthey ordered a base of fire to the front for about a minute to see if it would bring return fire. There was no return fire. Everything was deadly quiet. He sent the senior medic into the ditch to take a look and prepare Torres for a dustoff. Randy brought us up to the platoon CP and motioned for us to sit down.

He sat down with us and said, "It's starting to get light but I don't want you guys to go down there to get your stuff until I tell you. Okay?"

We had seen this many times before. If possible, they would send somebody who didn't know the KIA to assist in the dustoff. I was glad and I know Haggerty was too. We didn't want to see Torres that way.

The medevac chopper arrived and set down inside the perimeter and a minute later it was gone with our friend. Once again that empty feeling set in. It was almost like this never happened and Torres never was. I guess it's a form of shock or maybe it's the mind's way of handling something terrible.

A log ship came in with a hot meal, mail, and supplies. I couldn't eat and I didn't want to read my mail. I was very depressed and had nothing to say. I grabbed a cup of hot black coffee and just sat and wondered what was next. Randy told us that they had found the pin for the grenade that killed Torres and that one of his grenades was missing. He must have tried to throw it and dropped it and then tried to pick it up. If he had just jumped out of the ditch, he would've been okay. I couldn't imagine Torres making that kind of mistake. He was so careful.

We continued to operate around Binh Duong. Everyone seemed jumpy and quiet to an extreme. Nothing much was going on but intelligence was convinced that the enemy was in the area. We went from village to village searching and questioning. The villagers in this part of the province were mostly VC sympathizers so there wasn't much information from them. If they offered anything, it was whatever they had been told to say. Each day that passed, the weather seemed to be getting hotter. Two canteens of water had to get you through the day and carrying a heavy load created a constant thirst and made rationing even harder.

A few days passed and we had set up for the night in a cemetery. It was on high ground so there was a good field of vision and the enemy couldn't see our positions as we dug in. I had two new troopers with me and I was trying to give them a quick education on our nightly routine. They seemed like good guys. They listened intently as I explained what they could expect and what I expected from them. The most important thing for me to convey to them was that we needed each other. We had to be a team. I never got into that FNG (f...in' new guy) thing and I really don't think anyone else in our platoon did either. I remembered how I was treated when I came in and I had a lot to learn and everyone had a good attitude. I was convinced that the quicker these guys became part of the team, the better off we would all be.

I set up our guard shifts and I decided that it would be best for them to go first and I would take third and last shift. It seemed to be a quiet uneventful night. We rolled through our shifts and I was awakened for the last shift which would bring us into daylight. I sat on the backside of the foxhole and stared out to my front. It was beginning to get light and I could make out some of the terrain. I could see the green grassy terraces below and a thick tree line in the distance. As I looked out, I thought I saw movement about two hundred yards out. I focused on the spot and watched and waited. Before long, I saw a conical hat come up and then disappear a moment later. I flipped the safety off my M16 and aimed in the direction of the hat. After what seemed a long time, the hat came up again and I took aim and gently squeezed the trigger. The rifle cracked in the silence of the morning and I saw the hat fly. I continued to watch but I saw no more movement of any kind.

The two guys that were sleeping were now at my side and nervously asking me if we were being attacked. I told them that I didn't know but to train their rifles about two hundred yards to our front and watch for movement. Randy came to our position and asked me who fired and why. I told him what I had done.

He said, "Did ya get him?"

I said I wasn't sure but I saw the hat fly off and there had been no movement since. We didn't know what to expect next. We stared out to our front and waited. Randy decided to wait until it was completely light to descend the terraces and investigate. It would be stupid to try to go down with no cover. It would be the perfect trap.

Lt. Gibbons and one of his squads came to our position. He set up an M60 machine gun in our position for cover fire and quizzed me about what had happened and what I had seen. I pointed out the position and told him that I could lead the way. The Lieutenant and I and the rest of his squad started to work our way down to where I had seen the VC. We tried to move as quickly as we could because we had no cover and we didn't know what we might be walking into.

When we got down to where I had seen the VC, we could see that it was an old artillery shell hole. I picked up rock and motioned to the lieutenant and then I tossed it into the shell hole. Nothing happened. I flanked the hole and looked in and I saw the body of a VC soldier. He was dead. My shot had hit him in the temple and most of his head was gone. Lt. Gibbons jumped in the hole with the body and started to search it. The rest of us maintained a watch in case there was more VC. Lt. Gibbons came out of the hole with an SKS rifle and some papers. He walked over to me and handed me a silver Montagnard bracelet.

"Here. That poor old farmer you just killed would want you to have this," he said laughingly in his heavy Bostonian accent.

"By the way, Powers, that was a pretty good shot," as he looked up toward my position.

"Seriously, I think our friend Charlie was a scout and probably following us. I've got to take these papers to Hung for a translation," he said.

Randy came down and took a look around and said, "Good shot, Powie."

I never went near the VC body. I had seen enough and I didn't want to burn the sight into my memory. It was enough that I got him but taking a life is not something to celebrate even if it's justified.

We made our way back to our perimeter. The two new guys were right on us with a battery of questions. I let Randy do all the explaining. The incident had made them very nervous and they wanted to know if this happened all the time. Randy did his best to calm them down by telling them that we don't get probed or followed that often. In all honesty, I think that it made me just as nervous but I knew that there was nothing that could be done about it. Things like this bothered me no matter how long I had been in Vietnam. It was the uncertainty of it all or being in the wrong place at the wrong time. Sometimes it was just as simple as that and soldiering skills didn't matter.

Lt. Gibbons brought the VC papers to Sgt. Hung and the CO and he verified that the papers were an itinerary of where we had been and our movement direction and strength. S2 was interested in the papers and wanted to go over them so they were sending a chopper to pick up the captured rifle and papers. We would be holding our position until this was accomplished. The CO told the platoon leaders that battalion might change our mission depending on what was deciphered from the papers that we had captured.

The company was getting low on C rations so the CO ordered a log ship from LZ English with a resupply. This meant a mail call as well and that would be a good distraction from the morning's events. The log ship arrived and was loaded with supplies. We even got a 201 ration which would have fresh cigarettes, candy, shave cream, razors, toothpaste and brushes, soap, paper and pens. We were in need of all these things so it was a nice surprise. There was also a huge bladder of water dropped off. This meant a shave and a whore's bath for us. We used our steel pots for wash basins and I got right to the business of cleaning up. It felt amazingly good to shave, wash my face, hands and feet and put on clean socks and foot powder. As small as these things might seem, they were huge under these circumstances.

We had a hot meal and coffee and mail call followed. I got several letters from home and I couldn't wait to read them. Mail was our only link to the real world and escape from the reality of this hellhole. I savored every written word in those letters and tried to picture in my mind all the events that were in them. I tried to place myself there no matter how briefly. I longed for the day that I would return and vowed to myself that I would always appreciate the little things in life that we so often take for granted. One thing that this war and place did for me was to make me think about how great it was at home and to be out of harm's way.

Afternoon came and still we had no word on our next mission. I made good use of the time by responding to my mail. I wasn't a very good letter writer in the sense of content. I really didn't know what to say but I did know what I didn't want to say. I tried hard to avoid negativity and I didn't like to write if I was depressed. I guess I tried to mask how I really felt and wrote what I thought people wanted to hear. I always wanted to do what was expected of me and never wanted to convey any other thoughts.

The word filtered down that we would be staying in this location for a couple days while battalion evaluated the situation. Two recon patrols would go out each day to see if there was any evidence of the enemy being in the area. The patrols would return by late afternoon and the company would establish a tight perimeter for nightfall. I got some good news at this point. Randy had chosen me to be his RTO. This was the best job in the platoon. My load would be cut down considerably and that would help the problem that I was having with my lower back and I would get more sleep. My main function at night would be to monitor the radio. The down side was that when we were on the move, the radio would make me a target but I could live with that or at least I hoped so.

CHAPTER 17

The End of the Line

I really liked my new job. I got together with the other RTO's and got a crash course on the do's and don'ts of the job. I knew all these guys and they were quick to assist me in the learning process.

One of the guys gave me a neat little plastic laminated card with all the letter coding and all the battalion and company call signs. They taught me how to adjust the antenna which basically was how to obscure it when you didn't need the receiving signal as strong. There wouldn't be too many times when I would have to be on battalion frequency so I could keep the antenna looped down most of the time. The squad radio would be mostly inter company commo.

Randy was fun to be around. He liked to laugh and his face was very expressive when he talked. He would tell it like it was and he wasn't a kiss ass. I felt a lot of common ground with him and the other guys in our squad. Carrying the radio for Randy put me in the know for what was going on and I liked that. The radio kept my mind busy and there was less time to think about the bad.

After a few days in the cemetery, we were air assaulted into I Corps. This was Quang Ngai Province and the civilians were not considered "friendlies." There were many booby traps of all different types. It was a known fact that they were made and planted by women and children. Pacification efforts in this area had not been very successful and it was a sanctuary for the enemy. This area would remain problematic for the entire Vietnam War.

We landed at LZ Bronco near Duc Pho and immediately descended into the surrounding valley for search and destroy operations with our sister companies. Units from the 3rd Marine Division were operating along the coastal waters to our east and the 502nd Regiment of the 101st Airborne Division was sweeping the highlands to our west.

On our second night in the Duc Pho area, another tragedy occurred. In the early morning hours, a trooper from the 2nd platoon got up from his sleep to relieve himself. He must have been disoriented because he wandered outside the perimeter. While he was returning he was killed by friendly fire from his own platoon. It was one of his closest friends that fired the fatal automatic burst that killed him. The trooper that fired the rounds was devastated. I never saw anyone more upset; he was inconsolable. The following morning the CO called for a dustoff and they evacuated the KIA and his friend. There was no doubt this trooper was going to need a lot of psychological help. The past month had been a nightmare of perimeter incidents.

The next day, I fell into a small overgrown shell hole. The fall aggravated my back injury. I had quite a bit of pain in my lower back and the senior medic decided to send me back to Camp Radcliff at An Khe for some x-rays.

The CO was on the morning log chopper with me. I assumed that he had some paper work regarding the recent incidents. It was about a half hour flight back to Radcliff and I got a chance to talk to him. He wanted to know all about my back and I could sense his sincerity. He said he'd have one of the rear echelon people drive me over to 15th Medical Detachment. He said that when I was done over at medical, the rest of the day was mine and I could return to the field on the evening log ship.

We touched down at Radcliff and I caught my ride over to medical. I explained my injury and the on going problem to the doctor and he ordered some x-rays of my lower spine. Several x-rays were taken and I waited for the results. The doctor called me in and showed me the x-rays and basically told me that I'd just have to live with the problem. He said that it was just a minor strain to the discs in my lower back. I don't know why but I felt that he was feeding me a line of shit but you can't argue with captain's bars. At least, I could have a few cold beers while I was in camp.

I walked over to the engineer's EM club and went into the cool of air conditioning. It was like being in heaven. I ordered myself a cheeseburger, fries, and can of Old Style. I hadn't had a burger and fries since I was stateside. Two engineers came over and sat down with me and we started talking about home. One guy was from Rockford, Illinois and his friend was from Kenosha, Wisconsin. We hit it off right away and we were swapping stories. We drank round after round and before I knew it, I was feeling no pain. I told the guys that I had to get going. I had to catch a chopper ride and rejoin my company. We said our goodbyes and I stumbled out the door.

Once outside, I realized that it was beginning to get dark and I had missed the chopper. I made my way back to the company area and into our platoon tent. I crashed on an empty cot and fell right to sleep. I was in a deep sleep when I was awakened by someone poking me and yelling at me. As I started to come out of the fog, I realized that it was the 1st Sergeant. He was screaming about me missing the chopper and he was going to see to it that I got an Article 15. He told me to get up and get to the orderly room and that the Captain would deal with me.

I got up and went to the latrine and splashed some cold water on my face and started walking up to the orderly room. I got almost to the door and I could hear the 1st Sergeant ranting and raving about me and what I had done.

Then I heard the captain say, "Are you finished, Top?"

Things got quiet.

"Top, there is no way I'm gonna write that trooper up for getting drunk and missing his chopper. That kid has been out there pounding the ground for over eight months and nobody's had a bit of trouble with him. I wish I had more like him and besides I told him to go have some beers. Now send him in here."

The first shirt came out with a scowl on his face and said to me, "Get in there. The Captain wants to see you."

I went into the orderly room and the Captain was sitting at his desk with a little goose neck light illuminating a bunch of papers in front of him.

He looked up at me and said, "Miss your chopper?"

I nodded.

"Drink too much beer?"

"Yes, sir"

"Go back to your platoon tent and sleep and don't let me catch your young ass drinkin' any more beer. Understand?"

"Yes, sir."

He looked me in the eye with a little smile on his face and said, "You make damn sure you're on that morning log ship. Now get outta here."

The next morning I was up at first light and in the make-shift outside shower. I shaved, brushed my teeth, and had a hot breakfast at the mess hall before the log ship arrived. When the chopper arrived, I helped load it and climbed aboard. We sat there with the main rotor whirling around and I saw someone running toward the chopper. It was the Captain. He jumped on and gave the pilot the thumbs up and we lifted off.

He looked at me and laughingly said, "Glad you could make it, Powers. You look a lot better today. What's the story on your back?"

I explained to him what I had been told by the doctor. The Captain said that my new job should help and to keep him posted if there was a problem. I thanked him for his concern.

I smiled and said to him, "I guess I over did it with the pain medication yesterday."

He laughed and said, "You sure pushed Top's button. Oh well, he's a garrison soldier anyway. He loves paperwork and Army regulations."

I was glad the Captain saw this guy for what he was. Usually a CO has a lot of respect for a 1st Sergeant. It was pretty obvious that he had this guy down pat. I knew this guy was a jerk the first time he came out to the field. He lasted a few days and just couldn't hack it.

He came to the field another time while a group of us were having Doc Vincent check our feet. We all had emersion foot really bad and we were looking for some relief. He gave us a demeaning speech about malingering. We looked at his sorry ass and just laughed to ourselves and with that he was back on a chopper heading to his nice conditions at Camp Radcliff. The reality was he couldn't make a patch on Sgt. Hare's ass. The good news was that I never saw him again.

We rejoined the company at a village near Duc Pho. I hooked up with my platoon and Randy filled me in on our latest mission. The guys were still in their positions from the night before. After some C Rations and hot coffee, we would be heading north east and continuing the valley sweep. So far things had been quiet but the 22 NVA headquarters was supposed to be located in this area. If that was the case, things could change quickly.

We moved out and began another day of humping the bush in the blistering heat. I kept thinking about that air conditioned club back at Radcliff and those cold beers. It was something nice to think about and I needed that. You had to keep telling yourself that things would get better and that one day you'd be getting on that big silver bird back to civilization and a life.

When I looked around, there were a lot of new faces and names that I didn't know. B Company had lost thirty four troopers and over one hundred seventy wounded. When you considered that airmobile company strength was one hundred twenty five, you couldn't help but wonder if you were going to make it out of here in one piece. It was those kind of stats that you tried not to dwell on but as time went on it became harder and harder not to do.

We had been humping up and down hills most of the day when we got word that we were going to be picked up by chopper and relocated. We descended down a hill heading toward a small clearing that would be our makeshift LZ. The CO had already marked the LZ with green smoke so we knew the choppers would be there soon. We secured the LZ and we could hear the choppers coming. Our platoon would be on the third lift. Everything went smoothly and our turn came and we boarded the choppers and were airborne. The choppers banked and turned east and I could see the South China Sea. It was a short flight and I looked down and saw that we were headed for a clear hilltop. I could see the other platoons securing the perimeter as we came down and off loaded.

Our platoon assembled and all the platoon leaders and NCO's were with the CO. They were receiving their orders and soon we would be descending into the valley below. I was standing and looking out at the South China Sea and admiring the beauty of the coastline. The battleship New Jersey was a few miles out and I could make out the ship's profile. It was the 18th of May, a day I will always remember.

I was waiting for word from Randy when all of a sudden there was a tremendous explosion to my right. It felt like I had been hit in the head with a rifle butt. My ears were ringing and there was dirt everywhere. I didn't have any idea of what had happened but I knew that I had better find cover. I slipped my left arm out of the straps on my rucksack and I went to do the right and I couldn't move my arm. It was really strange, my mind told my arm to move but it wouldn't. I could flex my arm at the elbow and wrist but that was it. I extended my left arm across my chest and my hand into my right armpit and I could feel a large wet hole in my back. My hand was covered with blood.

By now, I could feel a lot of pain in my back and legs. There was something in my right eye. I knew that I was badly wounded. I could hear someone screaming nearby. I laid there waiting for a medic. I remember looking up at the blue sky and thinking that this was a rotten place to die and I couldn't even say goodbye to my family.

Luis Aragon, a senior medic, got to me and started working on me. I remember him telling me that I was going to be alright and that I would be going home. I didn't believe him because that's what they always said no matter how bad the wounds were. Sgt. Marcano was talking to me and assisting Aragon. They cut my shirt off and my pant legs up to mid thigh. I could see the holes in my legs. I had four wounds in my legs and they were pretty big and deep but surprisingly they weren't bleeding too badly. I could see the bone in my right leg.

The medic was more concerned with my arm and back. He got the bleeding under control and bandaged the arm and back wounds. There was a small piece of shrapnel in my right eye and he bandaged it so that I wouldn't be able to touch it. He gave me two shots of morphine in the legs for the pain. I asked Aragon what had happened and he told me that it was a booby trapped mortar round and that someone had tripped the wire. They started working on my legs and Aragon told me that a dustoff was on the way.

The guy nearby was still screaming and I asked Marcano what was wrong with him. He said nothing but part of my arm had hit him in the face and he thought he had received a head wound. He said they thought he might be going into shock and they were going to evacuate him with me.

The medevac chopper came in and there was dirt flying all over. The guys loaded me on a stretcher and slid me into the chopper on the floor. They slid another stretcher in alongside of me with a young trooper that I didn't recognize. The chopper started to lift off and I could see my friend, Jim Pitzen, standing there watching. I waved to him and he waved back and we were gone.

We were in flight on our way to LZ English and I looked at the trooper next to me. His eyes were open in the fixed stare of death but I couldn't see anything wrong with him. I looked at the onboard medic and pointed to the young trooper and he made the thumbs down sign. I didn't know him but I knew that he wasn't in Nam too long because his clothes were still pretty clean. Many years later, I found out that his name was Carl Hallberg and that he was only nineteen years old.

We got to LZ English and were off loaded at 15th Medical. I remember our moronic supply sergeant being there and taking my picture on the stretcher. I didn't like it and I told him so. He was another guy that never saw the field and probably needed those type of pictures to substantiate his bull shit war stories.

I was carried into a large GP tent and placed on the ground. The medics put an IV in my left arm and hung the bag on a pole next to the litter. I was really thirsty from the morphine. My mouth was completely dry and I couldn't have any water because they were going to take me to surgery as soon as possible. The best they could do for me was to wet a gauze ball and shove it in my mouth. It wasn't much but it was better than nothing.

While I was laying there waiting, I remember someone coming into the tent and apologizing for tripping the wire on the booby

Medics - Luis Aragon, unknown, and Ron Gow

trap. I can't recall his name but he was quite upset. I told him it was okay and not his fault. Sometimes things just happen that we have no control over.

Even with the morphine shots, I was in a lot of pain. The worst was my arm and back. After a while, two guys came and got me and carried me to another GP tent. They put me on a gurney and wheeled me over to a large stainless steel table and slid me from the gurney onto the table. The table was cold against my bare skin. I looked up and I was looking at a two lamp fluorescent shop light hanging above me. The medic set up the IV and a doctor came in.

I said to him, "When am I going into the operating room?"

He smiled at me and said, "You're there."

He picked up a syringe and inserted it into the IV tube and emptied it. That was the last thing that I remembered. I was in the total blackness of sodium pentathol.

I awakened in a hospital bed in the 85th Evacuation Hospital at Qui Nhon. I didn't remember being transported or anything for that matter. I remember a nurse waking me at intervals and having me breathe deeply and urinate. I came out of the surgical fog and learned that a successful surgery had been performed on my right eye to remove a small piece of shrapnel. The attending nurse showed me the piece of shrapnel that had been removed from my back. It was about three inches long and an inch wide. I could see machined threads at the end where the nose cone detonator screwed onto the round. It was from an 81mm. mortar round. The nurse explained to me that I wouldn't have survived if I had been turned 90 degrees in either direction. The fact of the matter was that looking at the South China Sea and scenery was what saved my life.

I had several wounds to contend with but the nurse told me that with time and orthopedic rehabilitation that I would fully recover. I was in a lot of pain but that bit of information was a pretty good pain killer. She explained all of my wounds and broken bones and where they were.

Her final punch line was, "Before you ask, yes, the family jewels are intact."

I had to laugh and I think that was her mission. She told me that I would rest for the day and the next day I would be transported to a hospital in Japan.

She injected a shot into my IV line and said, "This will help you to rest."

It wasn't long before I drifted off to sleep but I had dreams of what had occurred. I could picture Sgt. Marcano showing me what was left of my M16. The stock was shattered and the recoil mechanism was just hanging out. He said the PRC25 radio that I was carrying was destroyed too. I wondered to myself if those items had helped shield me from even more wounds or possibly worse.

In the middle of the night, there were two explosions and I awoke in fright. I had no idea if this was a bad dream or if we were being shelled. I heard voices around me and a medic was telling us what had happened. He said that Charlie had managed to get a couple rounds of 60mm mortar into the medical compound. He said no one had been hurt and he thought Charlie was long gone. Things quieted down and as I drifted off to sleep again I thought to myself, tomorrow can't come soon enough. When I'm airborne for Japan, I'm gonna have a smile on my face and pray to God I never see this hellhole again.

CHAPTER 18

7th Field Hospital - Japan

Morning came and preparations were being made for our departure. They brought breakfast to the ambulatories and I got a bag of something in my IV. Not too tasty I might add but they were concerned about me getting sick in flight. I didn't care what they did as long as I was leaving.

Two young medics came along side my bed with a gurney and a stretcher on top. They positioned the gurney and told me that they were going to lift me onto it as gently as they could. They did so but it hurt like hell. They rolled me through the ward and out the door into the sunshine. I couldn't see a thing because my eye wasn't used to the brightness. I felt like a mess. I couldn't move my legs and my right arm and had one eye for vision. My mind was clear of the drugs now so I was very aware of what was going on. I remember it being an emotional roller coaster, wondering how it would all turn out.

I was loaded onto a litter tram with other wounded men and we were driven out on the tarmac to a waiting C130 hospital plane. The plane had special racks on each side of the cargo hold and the stretchers were hung from the top to bottom and locked into the side walls of the plane. It took a while to load the plane and it was a pretty hot day already and it was even more uncomfortable in the cargo hold of the C130. I was glad when I heard the hydraulics whining as the tailgate lifted and closed. I felt the plane jerk as we began to move toward the runway. As messed up as I was, I was going to savor this moment. I was going to force a smile on my face as the plane ascended up, out, and away from Vietnam. I couldn't see anything but in my mind I saw and felt it all.

It was a pretty long flight to Japan, especially when you are on a stretcher and can't move. Every so often, a flight nurse would check on me and ask if I needed anything. She fed me drinks through a long straw. She put some pain killer in my IV and told me to try and sleep. I managed to doze off for a short while and that helped pass the time.

I was awakened by the plane's PA system instructing the flight personal to prepare for landing at Yakota AFB, Japan. My ears started to ring louder as we descended and soon I felt the touchdown and the braking action. The plane taxied and came to a halt. I heard the hydraulics for the tailgate and the sunlight came steaming into the cargo hold.

We were off loaded from the plane and onto air conditioned hospital buses for the final leg of our journey to the 7th Field Hospital. I was hung in place on the bus and I was right at window level. I would be able to see a little as we made our way to the hospital. I turned my head as far to the left as I could and I could see that we were passing through a densely populated residential area. It was a short ride to the hospital and my sightseeing was short lived. I can't say I saw much of Japan out that window but that is all that I would ever see of it.

At the hospital, I was carried into a ward and lifted off the stretcher and placed in a hospital bed. I looked around and I could see that the ward was actually a long quonset hut with beds on both sides and very close together. There was no one in the bed next to mine but there was someone across from me. He called over to me and asked me what unit I was in. I responded and he told me that he was in the 502nd Battalion of the 101st Airborne Div. and that he had got wounded in Quang Ngai. It turned out we had both been wounded in the same action only he was one day ahead of me. He said that we were in a surgical ward and that meant surgery would be forthcoming for me. We chatted for awhile and he told me about his wounds and that he was waiting for surgical scheduling with a specialist. I told him that I had no idea what was in store for me.

I heard voices and I saw a group of medical people headed my way. There were four doctors and several nurses with clipboards. The doctors removed all of my bandages and were examining the wounds and rattling off all kinds of medical terminology which I didn't understand. One of the doctors removed the bandage that covered my right eye and asked me a couple of questions. He said that I was very lucky with the eye wound and that the eye was healing nicely. He told the nurse that I wouldn't be needing the bandage anymore and said the blurriness would fade in a few days.

Another doctor who was examining my legs, arm, and back told the surgical nurse to schedule me for surgery the next day. It's kind of an interesting thing about being a patient in an Army hospital, they don't ask you what you think and they don't go out of their way to explain what's going on. You belong to them and they do whatever they have to and your thoughts and concerns are not part of the equation. You are government property, hence the term GI – government issue.

They departed as rapidly as they had come and they left one nurse behind to bandage me. She was a real sweetie and very pretty. She asked me where I was from in the states and we had a nice conversation while she bandaged me. She examined my overall condition and told me that she would be back shortly to give me a bath. She came back with a young male medic and she gave him instructions as to what needed to be done and to prepare me for the surgery the next day. He got me all bathed and prepped and he talked to me the whole time. By the time he got done, I knew his whole Army story. I knew that this was by design because there was some pain involved and it was usually when it was my turn to respond. It worked well and I was grateful. He cranked the bed up and asked me if I needed anything and said it was almost time for dinner.

I didn't get much for dinner because of the surgery. I got a little juice and a bag for my IV. This was okay with me because I was very nervous anyway. I had never been too fond of doctors and hospitals and I didn't even know what the surgery was for.

At 6am. the gurney rolled up to my bed and I was lifted onto it. The medics started to roll me down the aisle and some wise guy was humming taps and there was a lot of chuckling from the other patients. One thing about GI's is that they somehow maintain their sense of humor in rough times even though it's sometimes a bit morbid.

I was very apprehensive about the surgery. They prepped me and took me into the operating room and gave me the anesthetic and I was plunged into the blackness of sodium pentathol. I remember being awakened by a nurse in a post operation recovery room and being asked to urinate and breathe deeply. It seemed like I was agitated and just wanted to return to that deep black dreamless sleep. There was something so peaceful about it. After a while, I found myself back in the surgical ward. I was coming out of the anesthetic fog and I hoped that I was now on the road to healing.

Two days passed and everything seemed to be going pretty well. My leg, arm, and back wounds had been sutured. My arm was immobilized against my lower chest in a sling which forced me to sleep on my back.

The doctors made their rounds in the morning and they removed my bandaging to inspect the wounds. This gave me the chance to see my leg wounds. I had two wounds on each leg. Three of the four were large and located just above the kneecaps in the muscle tendon area. If these wounds had been just one inch lower, I would have had serious damage to both knee caps. I didn't have any bone damage to the legs and that was a big plus.

I couldn't see the wounds to the arm and back but the nurse explained them to me. I had a broken humerus and extensive damage to the deltoid and tricep muscle groups. I also had some facial wounds most of which were small. The more I thought about it the more I realized how lucky I was. If I had been turned 90 degrees in either direction, I would have had massive damage to the chest-lung area and that would have been the end of the line for me.

On day three morning, I noticed a stain on the sheet coming from my back wound. I figured that my bandaging had probably loosened during the night. The doctor came for the morning rounds and took a look at my back wound and discovered that it had infected. The doctor had me in a sitting position and he cut and removed the stitches and opened the wound. The pain was excruciating. He took a culture but that was just a formality, I could smell the infection. The VC liked to rub the surface of their mortars and mines with human feces and this would complicate the wounds with infection. The doctor told the nurse to have me transferred to the open wound ward.

This was a major setback because the wound would have to be purged of infection before it could be closed. I was about to find out how this would be accomplished. I was moved to the open wound ward.

There was a lot of activity in the ward. Medical staff were busy everywhere and supply carts were all over the aisle. I wasn't in the bed a half hour when a medic arrived with his cart to give me my first treatment. He sat me up on the edge of the bed and gave me some type of soft plastic to place in my mouth between my upper and lower teeth. I had no idea why. He mixed a solution of saline and peroxide and dipped a gauze scrubbing pad in the solution and began scrubbing my back wound. It hurt like hell and he was scrubbing so hard he was pushing me forward. When you feel pain like that, it is hard to gauge time. He finished the treatment and bandaged me. I now knew why the plastic was in my mouth. I probably would have broken some teeth without it. I never clenched my teeth so hard in my life.

These scrubbing treatments would take place three to four times a day everyday until the infection was gone. The cart would go from bed to bed and that would determine how many treatments received in a day. The first day I got two and I thought that was bad but the next day would be at least three. I couldn't eat in the morning or lunch because I was so nervous and hyper about the treatments. I tried reading but the words were jumping all over the page when I heard the clinking of the bottles on the cart as it got closer to me.

The guy in the bed next to me introduced himself to me. His name was Jon Davis and he was from McHenry, Illinois. He was a warrant officer and a chopper pilot in the 229th Aviation Battalion which was part of the 1st Cavalry. He had been wounded in the foot while in flight on a combat air assault. He was a real nice guy and a great talker. He had a good sense of humor and was always teasing me about being a grunt. Jon was exactly what I needed, a distraction from what was going on. After a while, I started to eat a little in the morning but I couldn't do lunch. Only after I knew that I was done for the day, could I eat.

I was able to read after awhile and I was doing a book a day. After dinner, the USO girl would come and show a movie and we would be issued a can of beer, two darvon, two aspirin, and two sleeping pills. I would trade the pills for a second can of beer. In the weakened state that I was in, two cans of beer and I was smoked and I didn't have any trouble sleeping.

The bandages were removed from my legs and the doctor seemed pleased with the healing process. The skin around the wounds was stretched very tightly and there was a little tearing by the stitches. I knew that it would take a lot of therapy to get these knees bending and to build up the damaged muscle above the knees.

It was over a week since I had been wounded and it suddenly dawned on me that I hadn't written home in two weeks. Before I got into a combat zone, I had instructed the Army that if I was wounded in action not to notify my family. I knew a notification like that would scare them half to death. I decided to write my brother a letter and send it to his place of work. I told him what happened and assured him that if I was able write a letter, I couldn't be too bad off.

I told him that I thought it would be best if he told our mother at home and in person. The last thing that I wanted to do was upset her. I gave him my new address and told him not to worry. It would just take time. I said that I was happy to be out of Nam and in a clean bed. I felt good sending that letter and assuring everyone at home that I was alright.

It was going to be a long road back but I was determined to do everything that I could to expedite it. I knew that my legs and arm had to be in good shape in order for me to return to my trade after the Army discharged me. I kept that thought in my mind throughout my entire convalescence.

I was getting mail now and this gave me something else to do. I was responding to each letter almost the same day that I received them. I got a card from the guys that I worked with at Westinghouse and they sent me sixty dollars that they had collected for me. I gave the money to a Red Cross girl and asked her to purchase every attachment for a Petri V6 camera from the PX. She did this for me and she was able to get me a light meter, a flash attachment, and a bunch of light filters. I had purchased the camera in Nam and it was in my duffel bag. It probably wouldn't be too long and my things would catch up with me and the camera would be a good diversion.

The personal effects that were on me when I got to 85th Evacuation Hospital hadn't caught up to me yet. I had over one hundred-fifteen dollars on me when I was wounded. I mentioned it to Jon and he laughed and said that I'd never see that again. I told him that I made them give me a receipt for it at the 85th. He said that I still would never see it and that this was a common story among the guys. Now that made me mad. I got the paper and pen out and wrote a letter to the commanding officer of the 85th and explained my situation. Jon was laughing the whole time and that just made me more determined to get that money. I posted the letter and hoped for the best.

A few days later, I had my answer. I received a small package from the 85th. Inside were all the personal effects and a check for one hundred fifteen dollars. I had an ear to ear grin on my face as I showed it to Jon and the other nay-sayers. I was very pleased with myself.

The days in the open wound ward went by very slowly and painfully. I had been in the ward for three weeks. Someone had told me that it would take three to four weeks to get the infection out so I figured that I was getting close. The doctor was working on Jon's foot and he told him that he would be going home to the states and hospitalized there. Jon was ecstatic and I was happy for him.

The next morning, Jon gathered his things and we said our goodbyes and he was on his way. I was a little down watching him leave and I wished that I was going with him. I was going to miss our conversations. Jon had a way of keeping me optimistic and he would watch as they scrubbed my wound every day and give me his evaluation as to how I was doing.

The doctor made his rounds the next day and examined my back.

He said to the nurse, "It looks clean to me. Close him up with butterfly sutures and air evac him to CONUS."

Those were the most beautiful words that I had heard in a long time. I was going home. I was going home to my family and my country, the good old USA! The doctor continued on his rounds and the nurse asked me what my hometown was. She said that she would try and place me in a military hospital as close as possible.

The next morning, it was my turn. I was loaded on gurney with a stretcher on top and wheeled out the door and over to a heli-pad where a medevac chopper was waiting. Several of us were loaded and the chopper lifted off for Yakota AFB. This was going to prove to be an interesting flight and not at all what I expected.

We arrived at Yakota and the chopper set down right next to a C130 hospital plane. This turned out to be my last flight on a huey. I don't know how many huey flights and combat air assaults that I had made while I was in Nam but it was a lot.

Air Force personnel transferred us from the medevac chopper to the C130. This led to some good natured kidding between the branches of service. A short time later we took off in flight but to my surprise we were headed to Clark AFB Hospital in the Philippines. It is about a four hour flight to Manila and the onboard nurses took good care of us. It was a nice smooth flight and after landing we were admitted to the base hospital. We learned that our stateside disposition would be determined here and that our stay would only be overnight.

I was in a nice clean hospital bed in a ward with very few troops. The nurses were all over us; they couldn't do enough for us. One of the nurses who was changing my bandages, noticed the condition of my feet.

She said, "I know you're infantry. I don't even have to ask. I'll be back in a flash and let's see what I can do with those feet."

She came back with a cart and went to work on my feet. I felt like I was in a spa. When she got done, my feet almost looked normal. We had a nice conversation the whole time. She wanted to know my story and I enjoyed telling her. I told her how excited I was to be going home. She told me that the nurses had a nice surprise in store for all the guys later that evening. I figured it was probably a movie or something.

We had a nice dinner and for the first time in a long time, I was able to enjoy it. After the meal, a Red Cross girl came around with the reading cart and I selected a couple of magazines to pass the time.

An administration nurse was making her way from patient to patient and informing them of their final destination. I was hoping for Great Lakes Naval Hospital but that was a long shot. She made her way over to me and told me that I would be heading for Ireland AH at Ft. Knox, Kentucky. She told me that the reason was because of all the orthopedic therapy that I would need and this hospital was geared for that. I wasn't too disappointed because Ft. Knox was only three hundred miles from Chicago. She said that we would be leaving the following morning and that I could expect to be at Ft. Knox within a couple of days. That was great news.

About nine o'clock that night, the door to the ward opened and two nurses were rolling a cart with a phone mounted to it. I was in the end bed so I was the first stop.

The nurse that had taken care of me earlier smiled and said, "You get one free call. Try and keep it as brief as you can so that everyone can get a call in."

She asked me for the number and dialed and handed me the receiver. I put the phone to my ear and I could hear it ringing. My mother answered and I could barely speak. It was so great to hear her voice again. She was so happy that she started to cry. I told her where I was and where I would be and that I'd call again when I could talk longer. That's all she needed to hear was that I was out of Vietnam and on my way home. It was really over.

CHAPTER 19

Ireland AH, Ft. Knox

The hospital ward came to life at first light. Everyone was anticipating the big flight and touchdown on good old U.S. soil. We had a nice breakfast and then it was the waiting game. I felt like a kid at Christmas. I just couldn't wait.

We were loaded onto a C141 Starlifter Medical Transport aircraft. This plane could handle eighty plus litters and was staffed with a doctor and nurses. On this particular flight, one half of the plane was used for litters and the other side for the more seriously injured who would need in-flight care. The litters were suspended from racks and when they hung me up, the litter above me was within inches of my face. It was a very claustrophobic and dark.

There was a young man right across from me that was attached to some sort of a wheel stretcher that was vertical and could be rotated. About every thirty minutes or so, the nurse would turn the stretcher 45 degrees. There was an in-flight physician by him almost the entire flight. I don't know what his injuries were but to say very serious would be an understatement.

The plane took off and we were on our way. I couldn't do anything on this stretcher. I couldn't even roll over on my side. I had to be on my back for the entire flight. The only thing that I could do was try to sleep or look to my left where all the seriously injured were. I felt so bad for the young man across from me. He seemed to be comatose and maybe that was just as well.

It seemed like we were in flight for an eternity when a nurse came by and made sure my strap was in place for our landing at Elmendorf AFB in Anchorage, Alaska. She said we were landing to refuel and we wouldn't be there long and our next stop would be Glenview Naval Air Station in Glenview, Illinois. Before long we were under way again on the second leg of our journey. The reason that we were landing at Glenview was to off load eighteen Marines who were headed for Great Lakes Naval Hospital. This part of the flight would be over four hours.

This was the worst part of the flight for me. When we were landing at Glenview, the pilot had to use heavy braking action because this runway was not designed for aircraft as big as the C141. We touched down and when we were braking, I slid forward on my stretcher a little and it was very painful because I was lying on my open back wound. The Marines were off loaded and when the tail opened, I could see the lights from the nearby community of Glenview. I was probably no more than an hour from home by car at that point. The young man who was attached to the special wheel was removed with the other Marines. The tailgate of the plane was closed and we taxied to the runway for takeoff. The pilot locked the brakes and revved the planes four engines for a power takeoff. When the brakes released, I slid in the opposite direction and felt more pain. The next stop was Wright-Patterson AFB in Dayton, Ohio for another drop off and then on to Andrews AFB in Maryland.

I thought that I would enjoy this flight but it turned out to be the happiest and the worst flight of my life. The flight ended at Andrews and we were admitted to the base hospital for an overnight rest and redistribution the following morning.

Once we were in the hospital, I was able with some assistance to get up on my feet. I couldn't bend my legs but I could shuffle along stiff legged pretty well. This was the first time I had been on my feet since I was wounded. I was very weak and I had lost a lot of weight but it sure felt good to stand up. I knew that I had a long way to go but at this point I was more optimistic about a full recovery. We settled in for the night and some badly needed sleep. I was exhausted from the flights. We had been traveling for over sixteen hours.

The following morning after breakfast, I was back on the stretcher again and the journey continued. This time I was loaded onto a two engine DC3 prop plane. This plane had one row of double seats and the other half was for stretchers. The plane had probably been a regular passenger plane and then converted into a hospital taxi.

Today's flight was to Wright- Patterson and then on to my destination, Ft. Knox. The medics placed my stretcher on the floor and strapped it down. My head was propped up on a pillow so I could look around a little. After all the litters were loaded, the ambulatories who would occupy the seating started to board.

As they passed me, many of them said hello and asked me how I was doing. A good looking young couple came down the aisle and took the seats across from me. I couldn't help but notice them because of their looks. The soldier was in his Class A greens and looked really nice. His wife was like a beauty queen. When they came down the aisle, I noticed that she was guiding him. It was apparent that he was blind. She introduced herself and her husband to me and we started to chat. She said they were going home to Ohio and that they had been at Walter Reed AH. She said they were going home to wait for the results. She looked at me with tears in her eyes and pointed to her eyes and shook her head no. I put my hand over my heart to silently say that I was so sorry.

We talked the whole flight to Wright-Patterson and I wished them the best of luck in their lives. She gave me a little pat on the shoulder as she stood up and they both wished me well. I had seen a lot in the past ten months but this couple was heart-breaking. They were both as nice as they were good looking. I couldn't help but wonder what was in store for them in the future.

The plane touched down at Ft. Knox and taxied up to within a few hundred yards of the hospital. Hospital personnel boarded the plane and began the off loading process. They lined us up on the tarmac and then onto gurneys and wheeled us toward the hospital. I remember what a beautiful day it was. The sun was shining and there were big white cumulus clouds in the sky. I felt glad to be alive. I wanted to get on my feet and walk into the hospital. I asked the male nurse who was pushing my gurney and he said that his ass would be mud if he let me do that. He explained that we were among the first wounded Vietnam returnees to this hospital and it was still a big deal to the senior staff officers.

As I rolled nearer to the hospital, I could see a multi-storied high rise building that looked to be fairly new. This hospital was supposed to be excellent for orthopedic surgery and rehabilitation. We went through the admissions procedure and I was placed in a four bed room on the seventh floor with one other patient. There was the number seven again and another numerical coincidence

It was a very nice facility and very well staffed. I got settled in quickly and I was scheduled for an immediate evaluation. The evaluation team arrived and reviewed my wounds. This time it was a little different in that the doctor included me in the conversation. After conferring about my arm and back wounds, a decision was made not to close them by suture but to let them heal from the inside out. It would be a slower heal but a better heal.

My legs were already healing and they removed the sutures. I was told that it would probably be a few weeks before any serious leg therapy could begin and my arm would even be further down the line. The only thing that could be done now was to work on my walking. I was scheduled for several sessions per day of assisted walking with a therapist. The walking would be done in the hospital corridors and outside when I was up to it and weather permitting. This would begin the following day.

A social worker came to see me and explained everything to me and answered my questions. She told me that the hospital had a nice PX on the main floor and that there were public telephones on each floor. She gave me a welcome pack that had lots of useful items including writing paper, envelopes, and other necessities.

I dashed off a few letters and watched some television. This was the first time I had seen television in a long while. I was enjoying a show when a young Japanese-American nurse entered the room and told me it was time for my first walking therapy. Her name was Lt. Keiko Hasuda She said that she would be my lead therapist the whole time that I would be at Ireland AH.

She began by examining my wounds and making notations on my chart. She was very nice but all business. She was going to get me going again and that was and would remain her priority. She assisted me in getting up on my feet and she grabbed my left arm and we began. My knees were flexing slightly and it hurt as the skin stretched where the sutures had been and the damaged muscles hurt too. She said we'd start slowly and walk to the end of the hall and then return. As we passed the public phones in the corridor, I asked her if I could come back later and make a call. She asked me why I wanted to use the public phone when there was a phone right next to my bed. I felt a little stupid but I didn't know that I was allowed to use it.

When we got back to the room, she showed me an easy way to get in and out of the bed. She said not to be shy about asking for help if I needed help to sit down. She gave some exercises that I could do in bed or if I was sitting on a chair. She cautioned me about not putting to much strain on the knees too quickly. I took a liking to her right away and I knew that she would be good at what she did because of her no nonsense approach. She didn't know how serious I was about my recovery. My whole future in the building trades rested on the outcome.

It was Thursday evening and I decided to call home. I called collect and my aunt Helen answered the phone. She was surprised to hear my voice and we got into a great conversation. She had come to live with us after my father died and she was like a second mother to me. My brother got on the phone and he told me that my mother and him would be coming down to Ft. Knox to see me on Saturday. That was great news. I spoke to my mother and I could hear the joy in her voice. This was the time that she had been praying for and her prayers had been answered.

Saturday came and I was really excited about my mother and brother coming. My bed was next to the window and I could see the hospital parking lot below. I figured that Ft. Knox was about a six hour ride and that I could probably expect them any time after one o'clock.

I sat in my bed and watched and at a half past one, I saw my brother's green Malibu pull into the parking lot. I watched them get out of the car and walk toward the building. I, too, had waited for this moment but I never pictured it like this. I always thought that the big day would come at the airport, not a hospital. A few minutes later, my mother poked her head into the room with sparkling eyes and a huge smile on her face. She hurried across the room and gave me a big hug and about ten kisses. My brother was right behind her and I got a handshake and a welcome home from him. My mother wasn't the least bit upset with my condition.

She looked me over and said, "You're too skinny but I can fix that. We've gotcha home now and that's all that matters. Everything will be alright in time."

I looked at her and thought to myself, she's always the soldier. No matter what you throw at her, she can handle it. We had a lot to talk about and plenty of time.

They had made reservations at a Ramada Inn just off post. There was a cafeteria on the main floor where they could eat and my brother had his military ID with him so they would eat at military rate. They stayed all afternoon and into early evening and they came back on Sunday morning and stayed until noon. They told me that my best friend, Fred, and his family would be coming to see me the following weekend. I was very happy to hear that and I told them that I would call and keep them posted on my progress.

Monday morning my therapy began in earnest. I had a whirlpool for my legs and the walking therapy four times a day. Each day the distance increased a little. Lt. Hasuda gave me a lot of encouragement and I could see that she was pleased with my efforts. I worked very hard all week long to ensure that I was making the most progress that I could. It was very painful with each step. The stretching of the knee was right on the wounds on both legs. The lieutenant suggested a couple new exercises that I could do in my room. By now, Lt. Hasuda knew that I was a construction electrician and that it was imperative for me that I regain my strength and the maximum range of motion possible. She told me that I had more determination than any of her other patients and that she could see my progress every day.

It had been a month since I was wounded. I thought to myself, it only took a second to do all this damage and a short time for the rest of my body to atrophy from lying in bed. I knew that this would take time but I had no clue as to how long.

By the time Saturday rolled around, I was walking pretty close to normal but I couldn't bend my legs 90 degrees. Lt. Hasuda said about one more week of walking and room exercises and she would start me in the therapy room twice a day. She said everything was coming along nicely and for me not to become impatient with my progress.

The doctors were watching over my back and arm wounds and seemed to be pleased with the wound healing but it would be awhile before any therapy could begin. Saturday was only a half day for therapy so it was up to me to continue in the afternoon and on Sunday. I was in my room sitting on a chair and trying to draw my legs up and into a normal position. This was very painful but I knew that it was helping and each try was a stretch on the damaged muscles.

I heard a familiar voice out in the hallway and I recognized it as my best friend, Fred. He looked into the room and saw me in the chair. He came over and threw a bear hug on me and then he realized that I had wounds and he started to apologize. I told him not to worry that I was okay. He had brought his wife, Floris, and their two year old daughter, Michelle, and his mother-in-law and father-in- law. Floris gave me a big kiss. I had been the best man at their wedding. I had met Floris' parents many times before so it was nice to see them too. We talked a mile a minute and I did my best to keep up with it all. It was really great of them to drive three hundred miles to see me.

After an hour or so, Fred started to heckle me as he liked to do and we were all laughing. He loved to get on me and try and rattle my cage. I do have to admit that sometimes he was successful but not today. I was so happy to see him and his family that nothing could have bothered me.

Fred was about six years older than me but for some reason we hit it off as friends. I had been hanging out with him since I was fifteen. He always said that I was very mature for my age and that

I looked older than I was. When we would go to a bar together, he would get carded and I usually wouldn't and that would blow him away. He loved telling everyone that he had molded me into this cool guy and I would just laugh at him.

I looked at Floris and winked and said, "Are you keeping him in his cage? You don't want to give him too much rope."

She laughed and so did her parents. We visited for almost four hours and then Fred said they were going to head down to Nashville for a day or two before returning home. I thanked them for coming and as we were saying our goodbyes, my good friend, Jim Kearney, walked in. It was like a changing of the guard. Fred and his family left and Jim and his friend, Bernie, and Jim's two sisters, Sue and Kathleen, arrived.

Jim said they had been down in the lobby waiting to come up for about an hour. He said that he wanted to surprise me so he didn't want the visitors' desk to call ahead. I was really surprised and glad to see everyone although I really didn't know what to say to Kathleen. I tried to act as normal as possible but I kept thinking about her not writing me. I wondered if it bothered her as much as it bothered me. We had some great times together and she had done a lot for me.

We were engrossed in conversation for an hour or so when an orderly came into the room and told me that my duffel bag was down in receiving and they wanted to know what to do with it. I asked Jim and Bernie if they would go get it for me. I was excited that the bag had finally caught up with me. Now I would have my cameras, civilian and military clothing, and other personal items.

Jim and Bernie left with the orderly and Sue went to the rest room leaving Kathleen and me alone. I didn't know what to say to her but I guess I was too proud or hurt to ask her why. She didn't bring it up either so I assumed there was probably someone else. I was mad and glad at the same time. I was a bit overwhelmed by all the company in one day and I surely wasn't prepared to see Kathleen. I was in a very weakened physical and emotional state.

I've never considered myself a vindictive person but as I talked to Kathleen, deep down I knew that it was over. Maybe it was the notion that I had been rejected. I appreciated her coming down to the hospital and I would always count her as a good friend. I sensed that there was something wrong with her but I couldn't put my finger on it. Several weeks later, I would find out.

Jim and Bernie came into the room with my duffel bag and I took one look at it and I knew something was wrong. The bag was about one third filled and when I last saw it, I could hardly get it closed. The lock had been removed and the bag wasn't sealed in any way. I asked Jim to dump it out and he did. There was a bunch of filthy clothing that had been used as a filler content. I could smell the clothes ten feet away. None of the clothing was mine. Jim started to put the filthy clothing back in the bag and he came upon the 380 automatic hand gun that he had given me before I left to go to Vietnam. The gun was fully loaded with a round in the chamber! I told Jim to make the gun disappear. The Army would frown on any type of a loaded weapon in the base hospital. Every single personal possession of mine had been stolen. The gun was the only thing that wasn't. My two cameras, a radio, and all my clothing were all gone. I had the Red Cross girl in Japan buy all the attachments and lens filters for the 35mm Petri camera and now I didn't have the camera to use them with.

I was so damn mad words couldn't express how I felt. What kind of a low life bastard could steal from their dead and wounded comrades. I remembered seeing a bunch of cameras on a shelf in the room of the supply sergeant's assistant. He didn't know I was in the storage area and he went into his room and left the door open. At the time, I didn't think much of it but I did wonder why he had all those cameras. Now I know why and now he has two of mine.

This little bastard was the assistant to our supply sergeant. He had a great job in the rear area at the base camp of An Khe. He never went to the field and never had to see and endure what we did. He got to sleep and eat in comfort and safety every day and this is what he chose to do. I would love to run into him one day but that's not how things work and true to form nobody ever said things were fair and that was true in the army as well.

Jim asked me what to do with the bag and I asked him to throw the contents into the nearest garbage container. Jim, Bernie, Sue, and Kathleen said their goodbyes and I thanked them all for coming down to see me. I told them that when my condition improved, I would be getting a convalescent leave and would see them then. They left and I thought that what had been a great day of seeing my best friends had ended on such a bad note.

CHAPTER 20

Convalescence

Monday morning came and it was back to the reality of therapy. Lt. Hasuda introduced me to some new exercises and told me that if I did well at them, she would have a surprise for me at the end of the week. I couldn't imagine what the surprise was but it was something to look forward to and make the monotony and pain of the therapy go a little faster. I really appreciated the interest and professionalism that the Lieutenant showed when she worked with me. I could see that she really liked her job and helping people. It seemed like she was genuinely excited when she saw me making progress and that had a positive effect on me.

I was beginning to get used to life at the hospital. I was able to go to the PX and the cafeteria on the main floor. I would occasionally venture outside the main door and sit in the sunshine on one of the park benches and have a smoke. It felt so good to be able to do something as simple as that. There were plenty of sites to observe outside. Ft. Knox was a busy place in July of 1967. Ft. Knox and Ft. Hood in Texas were the main armor training centers in the states and they not only trained U.S. soldiers but also the Allied troops. As different troops walked by, I could pick up on their foreign languages. They came to the hospital for physicals and any of their medical needs.

CONVALESCENCE

The weather was beautiful and I appreciated it more than most after being in the climate and conditions of Vietnam. As crazy as it may sound, I enjoyed the comforts and safety of the hospital. It was absolutely wonderful after a day of therapy to have an assisted shower and watch TV. Sometimes in the evening, a nurses aide would come into the room and give me a rubdown with oil of wintergreen and it was like heaven. All the fears of Vietnam were gone. Things like the darkness, attack, insects, snakes, hygiene, and sleep depravation were now history. I can't say enough about all these types of things that are taken for granted. I would never forget the physical and mental hardships that we endured and I would never again take these things for granted.

It is said that out of any bad situation, good can come if we look hard enough for it. I believe this is very true and it is something that I have always done and it has served to give me strength when I needed it most.

The week slipped away and on Friday morning, Dr. Ryan and Lt. Hasuda came into the room for their rounds. Lt. Hasuda had a big smile on her face and I had a feeling that there was going to be some good news. The Doctor checked the healing of my back and arm wounds and said that they were doing well. Lt. Hasuda showed the Doctor my range of motion improvement on my legs and had me show the doctor how well I could walk.

Dr. Ryan looked at the Lieutenant and said, "Well what do you think, Lieutenant, should we send this soldier home on a convalescent leave?"

She looked at me and winked and said, "Yes, sir. I think he's ready to reintroduce himself to Chicago."

I got a two week convalescent leave and was told that I could leave right after therapy this afternoon. I was excited about going home and seeing everyone. Lt. Hasuda gave me an exercise regimen to be performed at home everyday. She said that she expected my range of motion to be greatly improved upon my return to the hospital. She said that I would be starting therapy on my arm and doing leg extension exercises to build up my leg muscles. I gave her my word that I would be religious about her instructions. She went to walk out the door and she turned to me with a big grin on her face.

"Oh, and no sexual acrobatics either."

She was gone before I could respond and I knew that was her intention. That was the first time the Lieutenant had said anything like that to me and I laughed to myself. It dawned on me that I hadn't been with a woman since my R&R to Hawaii.

I didn't have to worry about packing because all I had was shaving gear. I would have to go down to the PX and buy a little ditty bag and some clothes to go home in. This made me remember my duffel bag and all the clothes that were in it. I was mad as hell to think that I had to buy clothes to go home in when I had civilian clothes in the bag that I had bought in Hawaii. I wasn't going to think about that again. I would just do what I had to do and make the best of it.

I went down to the PX on the main floor of the hospital and went in hoping to find something that fit me. I didn't even know my waist size. I had lost a lot of weight so I would need someone to measure me. I got one of the PX employees to help me. There was only one pair of pants that would fit and they were the ugliest shade of orange that I had ever seen. I found a shirt to match and some incidentals. I was going to look like an orange popsicle in this outfit but I have to say that I didn't care. I was going home.

I took my new found treasures back to my room and found an orderly to give me a hand getting dressed. He was a real nice guy. He not only helped me get dressed but he combed my hair which would have been hard for me to do left handed. I told him about going home for the first time and he explained to me that there was a bus that I could catch out in front of the hospital that would take me to Louisville Airport. That was great news. I thought about calling home but I decided a surprise was in order. I would grab a cab at O'Hare and just pop in.

I caught the bus and headed toward Louisville. It was late afternoon so site-seeing from the bus window would be good. The bus passed the Gold Depository that I had heard so much about. It was an interesting building. It was not at all like I had pictured it. The building was typical government architecture of limestone. The grounds were very neat, green, and shady. There was a small fence around the perimeter but I didn't see any unusual security. I had the place pictured with hundreds of troops all around it and all kinds of bunker emplacements. It actually looked peaceful and serene.

We went through a couple small towns on Highway 60. Kentucky was a pretty state. The rolling green hills and horse farms were very scenic as we made our way to the 265 bypass and on to the airport.

The bus rolled up in front of the terminal and I grabbed my ditty bag and went in. The terminal was small in comparison with Chicago's O'Hare. I spotted the information desk and checked to see what airline had the next flight to Chicago. I showed the young man my military ID and told him I'd like a standby flight but if none were available, I was willing to pay full price to get on the next flight.

He told me that I would have to be in uniform in order to get military standby. I explained my situation to him and he could see that my arm was in a sling.

He looked at me with a smile and said, "I think I'm going to have to make an exception for you and I really think that you deserve it. There is a Delta flight leaving here at 6:30 and I'm pretty sure that I can get you onboard. Let me talk to my friends over at Delta and see what I can do."

I thanked him and took a seat nearby.

I was embarrassed about how I must have looked in the orange pants and shirt and brown hush puppy shoes. I was trying to act as inconspicuous as possible but I really felt that I couldn't help being noticed. A few minutes passed and the young man called me back over to the desk.

"Gotcha covered on that Delta flight. See Tyler over at Delta and he'll square you away. Oh by the way, I'm an ex-Marine and I appreciate what you've been through in Nam."

I thanked him for all his help.

It was nice to hear what the man said especially after hearing about how some of our troops had been mistreated at airports by protesters. I don't know how anyone could do these things to those who have sacrificed and suffered so much. If they had a problem with Vietnam, they should take it up with L.B.J. and Congress. We were only doing what our country asked of us.

I went over to Delta and hooked up with Tyler. He was a gray haired gentleman with a big easy smile. He said that he didn't see a problem for me getting on the 6:30 flight. I paid the standby rate and thanked him.

The flight was short. The take off and landing took more time than the flight. The plane touched down and taxied to the terminal and I was on my way. I hailed a cab and hopped in. I couldn't wait to get home and surprise everyone.

I got into a conversation with the cabbie and I told him about my surprise return. He was a Korean veteran so he related to what I was doing. The ride seemed really short. We talked Army all the way. He wanted to know what I thought about the war and Vietnam. We both were of the opinion that it was similar in cause to the Korean Conflict. We felt that the US and its allies were fighting to prevent the "domino effect" in Asia. The cab rolled up in front the house and I went to pay the cabbie and he wouldn't take the money.

He said, "The ride's on me, soldier. Good luck and God bless."

I couldn't thank him enough. This had turned out to be the best travel experience that I could've imagined.

The cab pulled away and I was standing in the middle of the street looking at the house. My mother, my aunt Helen, and two of the neighbors were sitting out in front on the porch. They were all looking at me but not recognizing me. I smiled at them and started to walk toward them.

I heard my mother say, "Oh my God, it's Bob!"

There were countless hugs, kisses and well wishes from all.

We sat and talked for hours. They were firing questions at me faster than I could answer them but I didn't mind a bit. This was the moment that I had been waiting for. I was home at last.

I looked at my mother and said, "Do you remember what I said when I left for Vietnam?"

She nodded.

"This is exactly the way that I wanted it to be." I saw tears in those sparkling blue Irish eyes of hers and I knew they were tears of joy. I knew what she had gone through as a mother for the last year and now it was over.

CONVALESCENCE

We went into the house and I went from room to room looking at everything and enjoying the sight of all these familiar objects. I saved my room for last. I went in and it was just as I had left it. I looked at my bed and thought how much I was going to enjoy sleeping in it once again.

My mother insisted on making me something to eat and her and my Aunt Helen sat with me and had their nightly cup of tea. I gave my mother a little plan of how I would be spending the leave time. She wanted to know if she should take time off from work to take care of me and I assured her that wasn't necessary. I explained that the main part of my recovery was now in my hands and I had to continue it while I was at home.

I didn't sleep very well my first night. I guess all the excitement of coming home so unexpectedly took its toll. I was awake at first light. I got up quietly and made myself a cup of instant coffee and went out in the back yard. It was so peaceful and serene here. My mother and brother were flower lovers and I could see that this year was no different from so many others that I had known. The difference for me now was that I saw and appreciated the beauty in living things. I walked around the yard inhaling the scent of all types of beautiful flowers. We don't know what we have until we've lost it and to regain it is a piece of heaven.

I heard a voice from the back porch window.

"Hey soldier what are you doing out there? C'mon in and let me cook you some breakfast. Your brother's on his way to the bakery for some of that cherry coffee cake you like so much."

I think I could have had SOS (shit on a shingle) for breakfast and I would've been totally happy.

Saturday morning around the kitchen table is one of my fondest memories. We talked and ate. My mom gave me the latest on all our neighbors and my friends. She told me that while I was gone, my friends were stopping by all the time to see how I was doing and find out if I needed anything. My mother always loved company and the door was always open to those who wanted to visit.

I asked my brother about my car and he said it was ready to roll. He said that he had the car checked over by our mechanic, Bill Eddy, and everything was okay. He had the oil changed and filled it with gas. I couldn't wait to walk down to the garage and fire up that 389 Pontiac and drop the top and cruise. I planned on driving back to Ft. Knox and stashing the car in the hospital parking lot. In order to bring the car on post, it would have to pass a rigorous safety inspection to include seat belts which the car didn't have. I figured that I could get away with a visitor's pass while I was in the hospital. I knew better than to ask about vehicle registration.

My brother and I walked to the garage and he lifted the overhead door and there were our cars. He had a new green Chevy Malibu sport coupe and I had my Pontiac Catalina convertible that was a light metallic orange called Dawn Fire Mist. The car was six years old but it looked new. My brother backed the car out of the garage and put the top down.

He said, "What do ya think, can you drive with your arm in the sling?"

I said, "I damn sure can and I'm about to give you a demonstration. Hop in."

It was a thrill to drive again. We drove all over the neighborhood, stopping along the way to say hi to anyone that I knew.

Everyday was like a new adventure for me. I had so many people to call and all of them wanted to get together with me. I was not up to a lot of partying. I found that I became very nervous when there were too many people around. I was much more comfortable with less people and a quiet surrounding. I was surprised at this but I attributed it to the trauma and maybe the quiet at the hospital for so long. I realized that there was some emotional damage that I had to deal with. I felt that the best way to handle it was to go forward slow and easy so I put some limits on myself and my activities.

Being at home among family and friends was the best emotional therapy that I could have. It gave my mind a chance to push the physical and mental fears and combat memories to the rear. I knew that it would just be a matter of time before I would return to a normal life. It reinforced my conviction that I had to work as hard as I could with my therapy at home as well as the hospital.

Several days of reunions with friends and family made my two week leave seem like two days. The last day of my leave came and I made preparations to return to Ft. Knox. I was looking forward to the drive back to the hospital. It was a nice leisurely drive right down I-65 through Indiana. It was about a six hour drive. My mother cooked me my favorite corned beef and cabbage dinner and made me a nice sandwich for the road. I liked the idea of driving straight thru; the only stop that I'd make was for fuel.

I pulled into the hospital parking lot about 8:30. I selected a parking space that could be seen from my room. I hoped that the MP's wouldn't notice the car and check out the registration. Later I found out that they didn't check because Ft. Knox was an open post. I wasn't considered permanent party at Ft. Knox but temporarily assigned to the hospital.

I got up to my room and settled in for the night. I was tired from my drive and all the activity on my leave. I found out that my body wasn't as strong as I thought. I needed an exercise program along with my therapy.

The next morning, Lt. Hasuda brought me my new therapeutic schedule. She introduced me to some exercise machines for leg extension exercises and then she referred me to the shoulder and arm therapist. The lady who was handling this part of my therapy was a civilian. Her name was Sarah West. I took an instant liking to her. She had a happy looking face and a gentle way about her and a great personality. She loved to tease and joke and could take your mind off your problems.

She removed my sling and straightened my arm at my side. She had me bend at the waist and place my left forearm on a bench. My injured arm was now hanging straight down. She explained that I would be doing Codman exercises to regain strength and range of motion in my shoulder. The idea was to try to move my arm in repetition in all directions and in both circular directions. I could barely move my arm an inch in any direction. She must have seen the anguished look on my face.

"Bob, don't be discouraged. Your arm hasn't been functional in many weeks and this is just your starting point. I have seen much worse and I assure you that it will be just fine. Every day that passes, you will see progress."

I was told in the afternoon to report to a financial office to get my pay. I hadn't been paid in two months. I went to the office and when I received my pay, I noticed it was at an E-3 pay grade. I told the paymaster that I was an E-4 and he looked through my finance records and said that there were no orders indicating a promotion to that pay grade. Now that really pissed me off. Apparently, my paperwork from the 7th Cavalry had never gone through. Here I was sixteen months in the Army and still an E-3. I had a flawless record and I had been in combat for nine months. There was no reason for this. I really had a case of the red ass. I went back to my room talking to myself.

The next day, I had to go before a physical evaluation board. I had no idea what this was all about. There were a bunch of doctors sitting at a table. One of the doctors, Major Hickey, took my hospital top off and was showing the other doctors my back and arm wounds. He was running his finger over my wounds around my armpit in a zig-zag manner and talking in medical lingo that I didn't understand. I got the impression that they were talking about giving me a medical discharge from the army.

The next morning a surgical nurse appeared and started giving me instructions on my upcoming surgery. I explained to her that there was some kind of mistake. I wasn't having any surgery and that I was in recovery therapy. She said there was no mistake but she would check with the doctor and let me know.

The nurse returned with the same doctor who had conducted my medical evaluation.

The doctor, Major Hickey, said to me, "Is there some kind of a problem? You are scheduled for surgery tomorrow."

I told him that I was done with surgeries and that I was in therapy for my arm.

He said, "You agreed to the surgery and I was going to see that you received a medical discharge from the Army."

I told him that I didn't agree to any more surgery and I didn't want any more.

He yelled at me, "You're a fu..in' baby. You'll get your fu..in' way and I'll see to it that you stay in the Army until your very last day. You'll get no early out."

With that, he stormed out of the room and I was standing there speechless.

The more I thought about the way that jerk had talked to me, the madder I got. I would've loved to have wrapped that stethoscope around his neck until his eyes popped out. This had been one rotten day between my lost pay grade and this ignorant bastard of a doctor.

The next morning, I went down to therapy and Lt. Hasuda called me into her office. She looked at me with a little smile on her face.

"I hear you had quite a run in with Major Hickey. He wanted to do a surgery to relieve the stretching for your arm."

I looked at her and said, "Lieutenant, I'm sick of being cut and I just want to keep making progress in therapy and get my life back on track. Do you think the surgery was really necessary?"

She replied, "I can't contradict a doctor. How much the procedure might have helped you is hard to say. Between you and I, I heard that some of the doctors at your evaluation didn't think that additional surgery was necessary. I can't really say any more."

She didn't come right out and say it but I don't think that Hickey was one of her favorite people.

I continued to work hard at my therapy and the next two weeks showed great progress. My legs were coming along fine and I was walking normal. My arm and range of motion was getting better. I was at 50%. Lt. Hasuda was pleased with the progress and she set up a schedule for me that ran Monday thru Friday. I would be done early on Friday and I had an unlimited weekend pass which meant that I could go home every weekend. She told me that once I hit 75% range of motion, she would recommend a discharge from the hospital with a medical profile to return to light active duty.

August came and my therapy was progressing and I was nearing my mark. I couldn't lift anything heavy over my head but according to the therapists that would come with time. The muscles in the arm and shoulder would have to be strengthened with a heavier cycle of exercise. I was happy to see my range of motion back to 70%.

My car was getting a workout on the weekends. I was so glad to have my car at the hospital. After five days of monotonous therapy, I had Friday morning to look forward to. I enjoyed getting behind the wheel. The car was a dream to drive. It was heavy and held the road well and had lots of power. It was effortless at eighty miles an hour. Weather permitting, I could put the top down and enjoy the sunshine all the way home. It was during these pleasurable hours of driving, that I was able to do a lot of thinking about my future. It gave me a sense of freedom and peace.

1961 Pontiac Catalina Convertible

CHAPTER 21

Reassignment

The second week of August, the doctors, Lt. Hasuda and the other therapists concluded at my weekly evaluation that I was fit to return to light active duty with a U2 profile. A U2 profile meant no running, heavy lifting, or bearing of arms. I was told that I would be discharged from the hospital on Friday and that I would receive my reassignment orders at that time.

Friday's therapy gave me a chance to thank all the people that had brought me along in regaining my strength and range of motion. These people were very dedicated and I owed them. They had not only helped me physically but emotionally as well. I had a special thanks for Lt. Hasuda. She had been my counselor and mentor through all the therapy. I got a big hug from her and Sarah.

I went down to the administration office to pick up my orders. The civilian lady that was the administrator's secretary gave me my orders and she pointed to a large manila envelope on her desk.

"You are supposed to be decorated this afternoon by Maj. Hickey. All your service medals are in this envelope."

All I had to hear was that jerk's name. He would be the last officer that I would want pinning medals on me. I told the lady that I had an extremely important appointment in Chicago and that it wouldn't be necessary for the major to have a decoration ceremony for me. I picked up the envelope and went out the door before she could say anything.

I got into my car and took a look at my orders. I was being reassigned to the US Army Training Center at Ft. Leonard Wood, Missouri. I was none too happy with that. I pictured this as a basic training cadre of some sort. I had no interest in that but I also had no say in the matter. Ft. Sheridan in Highland Park, Illinois would have been a lot nicer. Oh well, the good news was that I was released from the hospital and I was looking at a nice thirty day leave before I had to report for duty.

I put the top down and pulled out of the hospital parking lot for the last time. It was a gorgeous day and I knew this was going to be a very special ride home. I-65 was a new road and it was a great ride. There wasn't much to look at on the inter-state but it would me home quickly.

I pulled up in front of the house at 5:30 just in time to see my mom walking down the street from the Rock Island train. She was toting a shopping bag and I knew that she had been to the Stop and Shop store downtown. She never ceased to amaze me with her goodness. She was always doing something nice. She spotted me getting out of the car and a big smile came across her face.

"Are you back here again. I'm gonna have to start charging you room and board."

I helped her in with her bag and I was right on time for the halibut and Spanish rice dinner that my Aunt Helen had prepared. I gave my family the news about my leave and reassignment. My mom thought it was great. Anywhere out of Vietnam, was fine with her. This was a happy time for her and I knew that she was enjoying every minute including all my teasing.

After a great meal, I looked around the Chicago bungalow kitchen that I knew so well and I thought to myself, what a great home this is. It doesn't get any better than this. I wouldn't trade this home for a mansion.

I called a few of my friends and told them that I'd be heading up to Johnny O's about 8:00 and I'd see them there. I walked into Johnny O's and I was greeted by a chorus of cheers. My friends had called a few friends and they called a few and the bar was loaded. Even the people that I didn't know wanted to be a part of the celebration. Johnny told me to keep my money in my pocket as he slapped a bottle of Bud on the bar in front of me.

The night flew by and we all had a great time. Johnny told me that he'd pick me up in the morning and we'd head out to the lake. He had a thirty-seven foot Chris Craft cabin cruiser moored in Jackson Park Inner Harbor. The boat was beautiful. It had the flying bridge with dual operating controls and it would sleep six. He kept the boat stocked with top shelf liquor and all the comforts of home.

The next morning, Johnny picked me up at 10 o'clock in his Buick Riviera and we headed toward the lake. He said that a couple of girls were going to meet us at the harbor. He teased me all the way to the harbor about one of the girls. He said she had the hots for me and we would have a good time. We arrived at the harbor and the two girls were waiting for us. Johnny introduced me to his girlfriend, Marsha, and her friend. Her name was Dawn. She was at the bar the night before. I had talked to her a little and she seemed real nice. She was a bottle blond and good looking with a body to match.

We boarded the boat and Johnny fired up the twin Chevy V8's and I cast us off and we were on our way. I loved the deep throated sound of those marine engines. The girls were seated on the back transom seat and I asked everyone what they wanted to drink. I went down into the galley and fixed the drinks. I came back out and gave Johnny his beer and the girls their screwdrivers and I sat down between the two girls with my beer. For a moment my mind went back to Nam. As I looked at these two pretty girls, I thought about how it was six months earlier. I had a lot to make up for.

We came out of the harbor and we headed north toward downtown Chicago. Johnny cranked up the speed and the wind was blowing through my hair and it felt great. This was life at its very best.

We stayed a few miles offshore and Johnny cut the engines and let the boat drift. We sat around drinking and talking and just having a great time. It was nice talking to a girl one on one again.

It had been six months since my Hawaii R&R with Marge. I was a little rusty but Dawn put me right at ease. Johnny and Marsha disappeared down into the cabin and shut the door.

Dawn stood up and took her blouse and slacks off. She had a white bikini on underneath. She was really built and I couldn't keep my eyes off of her. Dawn was smiling at me the whole time. I had never seen a girl so nonchalant about taking her clothes off in front of someone that she didn't know that well. I'm sure that she knew the affect that it would have on me and who knew what Johnny might have told her.

She took her top off and said coyly, "I don't want any tan lines on my boobs."

I laughed and told her that I totally understood. I didn't want to take my shirt off because of my scars. I was definitely very self conscious. We had a good time together but I wondered what she thought. I had a new issue to deal with and it wasn't one that I had thought about until being placed in this position.

We didn't come back into the harbor until it was almost dark. We all had enough to drink so Johnny put on a pot of coffee and we sat on the deck and talked until midnight. The girls had to get going so we said our goodbyes and that we'd get together soon and do it again.

Johnny and I closed up the boat and headed back home. He asked me what I thought of Dawn. I told him that she was nice but I had an issue with my scars and couldn't take my shirt off.

He looked at me and said, "You shouldn't even think about that. Let her decide whether she can handle it or not. Man, that's your 'red badge of courage' and besides you're gonna have to deal with it sooner or later. Listen to Johnny and you'll be fine."

I spent a good amount of my weekday mornings and afternoons with Johnny because he didn't have to open the bar until 4:00. Everyone was at work during the day so I gave him a hand with the boat and we'd sit in the harbor and talk. Johnny had lots of good advice. He had seen and done a lot in his life and I appreciated his advice. The only area where I didn't agree with him was women. He had the most negative attitude toward women and marriage that I had ever heard. A woman to Johnny was good for one thing only. I never knew what the reason was and I would never ask.

I kept a rigorous daily exercise schedule and my legs were pretty close to normal. My right arm was a lot weaker than the left and I knew that it would take a long time for it to be as strong as I wanted it to be. I was at about 90% range of motion. The scars on my legs, arm and back were horrible looking but I kept a positive attitude about it. I found that if I didn't dwell on it, it didn't bother me.

The leave time passed quickly. I got around to seeing everyone and I had a great time. Dawn and I hooked up several more times before I left. I have to admit Johnny was right. I had to let the self consciousness go and just let things happen. Dawn was definitely good medicine for me. She was totally uninhibited and she did her best to pull me in that direction. It would take time but I knew that it would happen.

I left for Ft. Leonard Wood on the 12th of September. It was all interstate highway so it was a nice ride. Missouri is a beautiful state and a fall drive into the Ozarks is nature's beauty at its best. I made the trip in seven hours and the car ran great as usual.

I reported to the replacement company for assignment. I was referred to a clerk by the name of Barton. His first comment was that he lived less than a mile from me in Chicago. He told me that he only had a month to go until his ETS date. We talked about 87th Street and our parish football teams. We knew a lot of the same people.

Barton said that he had three jobs available for me and that I could make the choice. All the jobs were in the 208th MP Company. He steered me toward a PX guard job. The job required me to carry a loaded 45 caliber pistol. He said that I would be wise not to push the fact that I had a U2 profile. He said that he would bury the profile in my 201 file and nobody would catch on. I agreed and thanked him for his advice. He gave me a little map to get to the 208th MP Company CQ.

I drove over to the 208th MP Co. and spotted the CQ building. I parked the car and walked over to the building. The post stockade was on one side of the road and the MP company area on the other.

All the buildings were WWII vintage. The company area was very well maintained. Even the landscaping was nice and that's unusual for an army post.

I entered and saw the 1st Sergeant sitting at a desk. I walked up to the counter and the company clerk looked up at me.

"Can I help you?"

"Pfc. Robert Powers reporting for duty."

The 1st Sergeant stood up and said to me, "Where the hell is your uniform, soldier. You don't report to my orderly room in civilian clothes."

I explained that I didn't have any military clothes and that I had no idea where they were.

He snapped at the clerk, "Patton, get him a clothing requisition for quartermaster and assign him a bunk in the overhead barracks. I'll go through his 201 file and make sure his story is true. And as for you, soldier, when you get your clothing, you report and sign in to this company in proper uniform. Is that understood?"

"Yes, First Sergeant."

I followed the clerk outside and he offered me a handshake.

He smiled and said, "I'm Hank Patton, company clerk. Top can be a bit of an ass sometimes but you'll have very little to do with him. You'll probably need a ride over to quartermaster. I can have Boyd take you in the CO's car."

I thanked him and told him I had my car with me. All I needed was some directions and the requisition slip. He took me into the barracks and showed me the empty bunks.

"Take your pick."

I made my selection and Hank filled out the clothing requisition form and gave me a little map to the quartermaster depot.

I drove over to the quartermaster depot with no problem and they weren't busy so there was no waiting. I got a duffel bag of new clothing, nametags, and patches. I waited while the patches were sewn on. I had to pay them to sew my CIB and combat unit patches on. I drove back to the barracks and put on a fatigue uniform, boots, and baseball cap. I walked back to the CQ.

The 1st Sergeant was at his desk. Hank got up and showed me the sign in procedure and went through company rules and regulations. The 1st Sergeant got up and walked over to counter and slapped my 201 file down.

"How many times have you been busted?"

I said, "None."

He came back, "You mean to tell me that you have been in the Army for eighteen months and been to Nam and decorated and you're still a PFC. I don't believe you. I think you've been busted and I'll find it right here in this file. There seems to be a lot of discrepancies in your records. If you've ever been busted, you better tell me right now."

I looked him straight in the eyes and biting my tongue said, "I have never been busted."

I left the CQ thinking about what a complete moron this guy was. It was hard for me to believe that he could be a 1st Sergeant. His name told the story, Oder, and he stunk.

My reassignment wasn't going so well. I was already off to a bad start and I wondered what was next. I unpacked my duffel bag and started putting things into the foot and wall lockers. I had a feeling that I better do things right and that I hadn't seen the last of Oder. He wasn't going to be happy when he found out that I had told him the truth and that he was wrong. He had made a big commotion within earshot of the CO and XO and hopefully made an ass of himself. I wondered if they knew what a jerk he was.

Hank came into the barracks as I was finishing my area. He said that he was going to take me over to supply and introduce me to SSgt. Richards. I was being assigned to him TDY (temp. duty) until my position became available. Richards seemed like a nice guy. He always had a smile on his face and he was easy to talk to. He mentioned my encounter with 1st Sgt. Oder but I made light of it. It could've been a baited question and I sure didn't want to antagonize Oder. He could make my life miserable and I sure didn't need that. Richards told me that there might be a change in plans and that I might be working for him. I thought I might be catching a break.

I finished the day in the supply room and went back to the barracks to clean up for chow. Hank came in and walked over to where I was sitting.

"Top came by and inspected your area. Everything was okay but he said you have to take all the combat patches off your fatigues. The commanding general doesn't allow combat patches to be worn on fatigues on this post."

I said, "I just paid the people over at quartermaster to sew them on. Wouldn't you think someone would've told me."

He shrugged his shoulders and walked away.

Hank came back a few minutes later and said, "C'mon, I'll take you over to the mess hall and introduce you to some of the guys. Are you going off post tonight?"

I said, "No, but why do you ask?"

He said that he needed to go to a laundromat and if I was going to Waynesville, he'd hitch a ride and buy me a couple beers. I told him I'd take him. This was one guy that I had to stay on the right side of and a couple beers sounded good.

I learned a lot on the trip to Waynesville. Hank explained the who's who in the 208th. He told me not to worry about Oder and that I had handled the situation well. He said Oder was impressed with my area and lockers and the fact that I had my bunk properly made up tight with hospital corners.

"In a week or so, he won't know you exist."

That in itself was reassuring and I needed that after today. Hank and I were friends after that and he was a friend in the right place.

The next morning, I was back with SSgt. Richards and he gave me a job straightening the supply room which was in need of some organizing. I'm a neat person so this was right up my alley. I wanted to do a good job for this guy. This seemed like a good inside job and I thought he'd be a good guy to work for.

At the end of the next day, Richards came up to at me and complimented my work.

He said, "I had hoped that you'd be working for me but you will be working for Sgt. Sundell. Report to him at the Provost Marshall's Office tomorrow morning at O8:00."

I was bummed. It seemed like "Murphy's Law" applied; nothing was working out.

CHAPTER 22

208th MP Company

The next morning, I drove over to the Provost Marshall's Office. The PMO is the post police station and the Provost Marshall is the top cop who is usually a lieutenant colonel. I walked up to the desk sergeant and asked him where I might find Sgt. Sundell.

He said, "Upstairs, second door on your left."

I started up the stairs and I heard a loud voice and some bad language. Someone was being thoroughly chastised. I got to the top of the stairs and realized that all of this commotion was coming from the second door on the left. I looked in the door and I saw a sergeant who looked like a bulldog. His uniform was impeccable and he had a chest full of ribbons. He looked to be Mr. Army, military creases on his shirt, spit shined shoes, and a shaved head. He glanced up at me and raised an index finger indicating that he'd be with me in a moment.

I took a seat and wondered where this was going. I was convinced this guy was going to make my remaining six months pure hell. It seemed that where the army was concerned, I just didn't have any luck.

The guy that was getting his ass chewed out, came out of Sundell's office with a face as red as a tomato.

"Now it's my turn," I thought to myself.

Sgt. Sundell called me in and told me to close the door and be seated. I noticed my 201 file on his desk and he was thumbing through it. I had a feeling that he had gone through it before my arrival and I wondered what Oder might have told him.

He looked me up down and said, "1st Cavalry, infantry, purple heart. Looks to me like you paid your dues. I'm infantry too. 7th Division, Korea. MP's are a bunch of pimps."

I couldn't believe what I was hearing.

He continued, "How come you're still a PFC?"

I explained my circumstances to him and he listened with interest. He asked me about my family and how I was readjusting to normal life. I had the feeling that he was sincere in his interest.

He told me what he expected from me, and said if I did the job as well as the guy that's doing it now, we'd have no problem. He asked me if I had met Don Johnson yet and I said I hadn't.

He said, "Johnson is due to get out of the Army in a couple weeks and you'll be taking over. I don't know exactly how the job works but you hook up with him and he'll show you the ropes. That's all for now, Powers."

I got up and started out the door.

He said, "I'll have your "bird" for you in thirty days." (bird is SP4)

I had no idea of how to hook up with Johnson so I drove back to the company area. I asked about Johnson and I was told that he was in the overhead barracks. It turned out that he was in the bunk next to me. I caught up with Johnson later that day and introduced myself to him. He explained the job to me. It was like being an armed guard on a small money changing truck. The two men on the truck that I would be working with were retired Army sergeants and PX employees. Two runs a day were made to all the post facilities to make change for them and pick up their bank deposits. It was about a six hour day. He advised me not to talk about the job too much because he felt that it was the best job on the post and there would be a lot of jealousy.

Johnson said that he would take me on the afternoon run and introduce me to Lou and Paul and show me the routine. The job was really nice. All I had to do was dismount the truck and stand at the rear while the doors were opened and make sure that nobody came near. There was a safe in the rear of the truck and bags of coinage. The two men would go in to each facility and make the necessary transactions and we were off to the next stop.

The two men that operated the truck were nice guys. When they found out that I was a Vietnam returnee, I was accepted and they treated me great.

Johnson told me the best thing to do was to avoid the company area so that no one knew my hours or routine, especially Sergeants Oder or Richards. If they knew the routine they would probably give me extra duty. He said Sgt. Sundell was the greatest and that he didn't care what the hours were as long as there were no complaints from the PX authority.

Johnson was very helpful. He told me who I could trust and who to watch out for. He said if I needed anything to go right to Sgt. Sundell and no one else. It turned out that all of his advice was right on the mark and I followed it to the letter.

Johnson's permanent home was no more than a half hour from the back gate of the post so when he completed work he just went home. He rarely stayed in the barracks. He told me if it was at all possible, to get out of the company area on the weekends because if any of the stockade prisoners escaped, the MP command would grab whoever was available to go out and beat the bush looking for the escapees. If you weren't around; you weren't involved. This was really important advice.

I doubled up on the truck with Johnson for a week and then I took over and established my own routine based on his advice. Things couldn't have been any better. I really enjoyed the job. I got to know the fort really well and all the PX facilities and managers. I knew when all the sales were taking place and what time to be at each facility.

I made a list of all the clothing and items that I would need when I returned to civilian life. The prices at the PX were super cheap and this would give me a good start when I was released from active duty. My day's starting and finishing points were the main PX. The end of my day was opening time for the main PX.

This meant that I could go in and have the best selection before the troops or their dependants arrived. I could be very selective about what I was buying and I had six months to complete my shopping. This would also keep me from returning to the company area too early.

Another priority on my list was dental work. It had been two years since I had been to a dentist. Fort Leonard Wood had a brand new dental clinic that had all the state of the art equipment. I decided that I would take care of all these kinds of incidentals before my discharge. I felt that I had a plan in place and that my time at Ft. Leonard Wood would be constructive.

The overhead barracks was comprised of senior NCO's on the upper floor and junior NCO's and EM on the 1st floor. It was cooks, motor pool, the company clerk and driver, supply, arms clerk, dog catcher, and PX guard. It was the perfect place to be. Anything you needed, you had. The barracks was also a quiet place. It was a good place to read and relax. I had a twelve inch television that I had brought from home and I told the guys to use it whenever they wanted, but surprisingly it didn't get a lot of use. Most of the guys were elsewhere at night, they wanted no part of the barracks.

I have to say that I enjoyed being in the barracks Monday thru Friday. It was all quiet time for me. The guys liked to go to Waynesville's bars and raise hell but that was gone from me. I did a lot of reading during the week and I was gone every weekend. I had a friend in St. Louis and I had a standing invitation for a Saturday over night visit.

I got real friendly with Lou, and sometimes after work we'd grab a six pack and go to his house. His wife was very nice and she always wanted me to hang around for dinner. They had three pretty daughters and I think that they hoped that I would have an interest in one of the two older girls. I could read between the lines and I knew this wouldn't be a good idea. Everything was going good for me. I had no extra duties of any kind. I worked about thirty-two hours a week at a job that was remote from normal army jobs. I didn't even have to clean my 45 pistol; Tony, the arms clerk, did it for me. I wanted everything to stay just as it was.

The time was flying by and I didn't realize it then but this was probably the best emotional therapy that I could possibly have. The jerk doctor at Ft. Knox who thought he was punishing me had inadvertently helped me. This quiet daily routine was just what I needed to help me put aside some of the horror that I had witnessed in Vietnam. When I was discharged from the hospital, I wasn't ready for civilian life. I needed this time and this job to make that transition. I was interacting with people every day and it wasn't an Army theme. I got a chance to see another side of the Army. Now I had seen both the good and the bad of Army life.

The weeks and months were flying by. Everything that I'd planned was falling into place. Charlie Moss, the AWOL apprehension specialist, had the bunk next to me. We became friends and exchanged favors. He would make my job run on Saturday occasionally. This gave me the opportunity to make a run home on a weekend and drop off my PX purchases.

I couldn't make arrangements for a Thanksgiving pass so my mother and brother decided to bring Thanksgiving to me. They came down for the weekend and we had Thanksgiving dinner in the 208th MP Company mess hall. My mom was so was impressed with the mess hall and its operation that she had to compliment the head cook. From then on, whenever I would see the head cook, he'd ask me how my mom was. I guess everyone appreciates a compliment.

I took her on a tour of the fort and all its facilities. It was a great time and a helluva difference from the previous Thanksgiving.

I was able to get a pass to go home for Christmas. There was a fellow in the barracks, named Mike Scanlon. Mike was from California and he couldn't afford to go home for Christmas. He was really down in the dumps and I felt bad for him. I made a call home and asked my family if I could bring Mike home with me for the holiday. Later that day, Mike and I were talking.

I said, "Mike, seeing how you can't get home for Christmas, how would you like to spend Christmas with my family in Chicago?"

"Oh, I couldn't do that. I couldn't impose like that."

"Mike, my family would be happy to have you and besides I already told them you were coming. You don't want to be sitting in the barracks on Christmas."

"I guess you're right."

"Well, then it's settled."

Mike was like a new man and I could tell he was really looking forward to meeting my family and friends and seeing a little of the "Windy City."

We drove up to Chicago and I introduced Mike to my family and all my friends. There were parties everywhere and, of course, my mother's Christmas dinner. We had a great time going around seeing my friends. I took Mike to some of my favorite haunts and showed him a little of the Southside.

He said, "I can't believe your family and friends. I've felt so welcome. I'm glad I listened to you. This is one Christmas that I'll always remember."

"I'm glad you came, Mike. Nobody should have to spend Christmas alone, especially in an Army barracks."

March came around quickly and I started the post clearance process. This was the time that I had been waiting for. I really wasn't as anxious as I thought I would be. I had enjoyed my job and the people that I worked with. I can't say enough about Sgt. Sundell. He treated me great and I would always remember him and all that he had done for me.

The big day rolled around. I put on some nice comfortable civilian clothes for the ride home. It was a Friday and the sun was shining. This was going to be one of the best days of my life and I had such a great feeling inside. I had accomplished my two goals in the Army: an honorable discharge and a good conduct medal.

All that remained, was for me to give my post clearance papers to the company clerk and pick up my separation orders and sign out of the company. Hank, the company clerk, had helped me through all the paperwork and made things a lot easier. I was sure glad that I had befriended him when I first arrived.

I went over to the mess hall and had my last Army meal. I said my goodbyes to the guys and wished them all the best. I went back to the barracks and packed my belongings into my car. I walked over to the CQ and went in. Hank got up from his desk and gave me my separation papers and took the post clearance papers from me. He had a big smile on his face as he extended his hand out for a shake.

"Good luck, Bob. It was a pleasure knowing you."

1st Sgt. Oder looked up and said, "Who the hell are you?"

Before I could open my mouth, Hank explained who I was and that I was being discharged today.

Oder said to me, "You're not signing out of my company in those clothes. You will sign out in a Class A uniform."

I don't know how I managed to keep my mouth shut. I wasn't going to let this asshole ruin one of the happiest days of my life. I went out to my car and got my duffel bag and went back into the barracks. I put my Class A's on and packed the civilian clothes into the duffel bag and loaded the bag back into the car.

I walked back to the CQ and went in. I signed the log book and looked over at Hank.

He shook his head and said, "Have a good safe trip home."

Oder never looked up at me. The door of the CQ opened and Capt. Nichols, my CO, walked in. He came right over to me and shook my hand.

He said, "Good luck to you, Powers. You did a fine job and you're a credit to the Army.

I thanked him and glanced over at Oder. His head was still down and I knew he was probably pissed about what the CO had said to me.

I got in my car and drove to the main gate. The MP on the gate gave me the halt sign and told me to pull over. I wondered what the hell was wrong now. I pulled the car over and I saw Sgt. Sundell come out of the guard shack carrying a black plastic garbage bag and a big smile on his face.

"You didn't think you were gonna get outta here without one last goodbye, did you? I got a couple field jackets and liners in here for you. I imagine its pretty cold for an electrician up in Chicago during the winter."

I gave him a strong handshake and said goodbye. I thanked him again for the way that he had treated me. He said that he only wished that he could've talked me into staying in the Army.

I got into my car and started down the road and I thought to myself that in the last hour I had seen the biggest jerk in the Army and the best sergeant in the Army.

This was going to be a great day.

Glossary

AK-47	Kalishnikov Russian assault rifle
ARA	Aerial Rocket Artillery, rockets fired from pods mounted on HU-1B helicopters
ARVN	Army of the Republic of South Vietnam, a soldier or unit of the So. Vietnam Army
Battalion	Tactical army unit made up of headquarters company, three rifle companies, and one heavy weapons company, approx. 750 men
Battery	A grouping of artillery guns for infantry support
Brigade	Next tactical unit size above a battalion
C4	Plastic explosive
C130	Turbo prop aircraft for cargo or troops capable of takeoffs from short or rough runways
C141	Larger jet powered cargo aircraft
Charlie	Viet Cong
Chinook	Large two engine helicopter used for Platoon movement or logistics
CIB	Combat Infantryman Badge
CIC	Counter Intelligence Corps
Claymore	Anti- personnel mine
CO	Commanding Officer
Company	175 men, 4 platoons

GLOSSARY

CONUS ....Continental United States
CP ....Command Post
C rations ....Field meal in cans
CQ ....Company Headquarters
DEROS ....Departure date
Dustoff.................Medical evacuation operation
EM.......................Enlisted men
ETS......................Elapsed time of service
Firebase or LZ ......Artillery position and landing zone secured by infantry, usually on high ground or hill
Field of fire...........A clear area for a weapon to engage the enemy
Fire team...............Primary maneuvering unit of a squad
FO.......................Forward observer for artillery fire Adjustment
Garry Owen ....Motto for the 7th Cavalry
Gunship ....Heavily armed HU-1B helicopter for Infantry support
HE rounds.............High explosive rounds from artillery mortars
H&I Fire ....Harassing and interdicting fire
HHC.....................Battalion Headquarters
High Angle Fire ....Indirect fire weapons such as artillery or Mortars
HQ ....Headquarters
Huey ....HU-1B helicopter used for gunships, log, medevac, and assault
KIA......................Killed in action
Klick ....One thousand meters
LAW ....Shoulder fired anti-tank weapon
L.B.J ....Lyndon B. Johnson
Log bird ....Resupply helicopter
LP ....Listening post
LZ ....Landing area for helicopters or temporary base
M16 ....American assault rifle
M48 ....52 ton American battle tank
M50 ....50 caliber machine gun
M60 ....7.62mm machine gun
M79 ....40mm grenade launcher

Medevac................Medical evacuation helicopter
MIA ....Missing in action
MOS ....Military occupational specialty
MPC.....................Military payment certificates
NCO....................Non-commissioned officers, grades E4 to 9
NVA ....North Vietnamese Army
Platoon.................47 men, 4 squads
Point....................Lead man or unit in an infantry maneuver
PRC-25 ....Principal infantry radio used in Vietnam
P-38 ....Small folding can opener used to open C
                      Rations
Punji stick.............A sharpened, hardened bamboo stick coated
                      with feces and placed on an angle in the
                      ground to inflict infected wounds
PX........................Post stores and facilities operated by Civilians
                      and non profit
R&R.....................Rest and relaxation leave out of country
RTO ....Radio telephone operator
S1........................Officer in charge of personnel matters
S2........................Intelligence Officer
S3........................Operations Officer
S4........................Supply Officer
Selective Service ..1A- eligible for draft, 1Y-school deferment
                      Classifications
Sit Rep ....Situation report via radio
SKS......................7.62mm semi-auto Russian rifle
Slick.....................UH-1B helicopter for troop assault
SOP......................Standard operating procedure
SOS......................Shit on a Shingle – chipped beef in gravy on
                      toast
Squad...................11 men, 2 fire teams
TC.......................Tank Commander
Tracer...................Phosphor coated bullets - illuminating
VC ....Viet Cong
WIA ....Wounded in action
XO ....Executive Officer, second in command
4 duece.................4.2 inch mortar

GLOSSARY

81 ....81mm mortar
105 ....105mm howitzer
106 ....106mm recoilless, usually jeep mounted
155 ....155mm howitzer

CPSIA information can be obtained at www.ICGtesting.com
Printed in the USA
LVOW062351121211

259094LV00001B/12/P